WHAT THEY'RE SAYING

Too many of us have gone about finding our livelihood in a haphazard way. Before long, we become a statistic in a job dissatisfaction survey. Happily, it doesn't have to be that way and Brian Cormack Carr proves it. If you think that work should be about more – much more - than just a way to pay your bills, this book is the roadmap you've been looking for. Work with How To Find Your Vital Vocation for a short time and you'll be working at your real work for a long time.

**Barbara J. Winter -
bestselling author of Making a Living Without a Job**

Warm, witty and wise. I highly recommend this book. It clarifies the mystery and practicality of discovering your career purpose and getting a job you'll love. Brian knows his stuff and How To Find Your Vital Vocation is a breath of fresh air.

Grace Owen – executive coach and author of The Career Itch

I appreciated the step-by-step nature of Vital Vocation. It made finding a new career that much easier, and I'm still amazed at how well it helped me clarify what I wanted to do with the rest of my life.

**David, member of the Vital Vocation Online
Coaching Programme**

Vital Vocation helped me focus after I had spent too long panicking and going nowhere. Now my part-time hobby has grown to a full-time occupation and I've finally given up the day job that was making me sad!

**Steven, member of the Vital Vocation
Online Coaching Programme**

It had never occurred to me that I could make a good living at a decent job and pursue my real passion as well. The Vital Vocation programme helped me to see that not only was this possible, it was a great way to create work/life balance. Now I'm making a little bit of money through my hobby too, so I have two useful income streams, which has been great for my sense of security, especially with the recession. Just brilliant!

Nicholas, member of the Vital Vocation
Online Coaching Programme

I had such a big decision to make in changing my job and starting a new business. Brian helped me to put my thought patterns straight and to establish practical steps to take. I've been able to balance what I need to do in order to bring in enough money to pay the bills, with what I really love and want to do long term.

Stephanie, Vital Vocation coaching client

Since working with Brian I have set up my business and I'm hopeful of a bright, successful and happy future!

Cynthia, Vital Vocation coaching client

"What's with the elephant on the cover?"
To find out, please see
Afterword: Questions and Answers.

This book is gratefully dedicated to:

My parents, Brian and Janet Carr, for their love and support through the years (and for always believing that they'd see my name in print one day)

and to

My partner, Pete, for his brilliance and patience and for knowing exactly how to make me smile, especially when things get "a bit much"

and to

The fond memory of my mother, Elizabeth Elspet Cormack Carr, who taught me that caring about other people is the most important job in the world.

You owe it to all of us to get on with what you're good at.

~ W.H. Auden

The only way to make sense out of change is to plunge into it, move with it, and join the dance.

~ Alan Watts

TABLE OF CONTENTS

PART ONE: FINDING IT

PART TWO: GETTING IT

ACKNOWLEDGMENTS

With grateful thanks to everyone who helped this book come to life:

All my coaching clients and the participants in the *Vital Vocation Online Coaching Programme* for their enthusiasm and feedback, and for encouraging me to turn this material into a book.

My blog readers, newsletter subscribers, Facebook fans and Twitter followers for their invaluable insights - and for voting in my "best cover" competition.

Jane Dixon-Smith of *JD Smith Design* for her artistic layout ideas and imaginative cover design skills – thanks to her, I'm now (happily) seeing elephants everywhere.

My partner and best friend Pete Lambert for allowing me to be the madman in the attic – and for giving me the space, time and support I needed to get all this down on paper.

Stephen Mitchell, co-author of *Loving What Is* and translator of the *Tao Te Ching* for his helpful suggestions for improving the contents of Chapter 8.

Grace Owen, expert career coach and author of *The Career Itch* for her support and advice – and for being such an inspiring colleague and friend.

Hayley Sherman of *Whoosh! Editing* for her expert eye and attention to detail, and for "test-driving" the exercises in this book – any errors remaining in the text are my own.

Barbara J. Winter, inspiring entrepreneur and author of *Making a Living Without a Job* and *Jump Start Your Entrepreneurial Spirit!* for making time to read and helpfully comment on the manuscript in its draft form – and for so generously being "the Quote Police".

It has been a privilege to work with and learn from such talented and interesting people. They each in their own way are doing much to help others find and live their Vital Vocation.

INTRODUCTION

It is not more vacation we need
– it is more vocation.

~ Eleanor Roosevelt

How I Found My Vital Vocation

"I can't do this anymore."

The words popped into my head as I slipped behind my desk again at Marks & Spencer's Leicester store, where I had been working – after a gruelling two-year graduate training scheme – as one of the company's personnel managers.

It wasn't the first time the thought had crossed my mind – in fact, it had been doing so with alarming frequency over the preceding months – but it did turn out to be the last.

Propelled by a conviction that seemed beyond my control, I put down my pen, took a shaky breath and marched along the corridor to my boss's office, where I resigned before I had a chance to change my mind. And before you ask, no: I didn't have another job lined up.

When I think of it now, I'm amazed at my foolhardiness. What on *earth* was I thinking?

It wasn't that I hated the job. In fact, there was a great deal about it I liked very much; I worked in a great company with interesting and talented people, the salary and benefits were generous, and the professional development opportunities were outstanding.

The problem was I didn't *love* it. It didn't feel like *me*. Somehow, I just couldn't get excited about profit and loss accounts, salary reconciliations, or increasing the sales in men's underwear.

Just a few weeks earlier, I had been visited by a senior personnel manager from head office. A formidable woman in her late fifties, immaculately presented - in finest M&S tailoring of course - she kept in regular contact with personnel managers in stores across the country and was corporately responsible for our welfare and career progression.

On that last visit, she asked me where I saw myself going in my career. Her face fell when I told her I wasn't immediately interested in scaling the corporate ladder into a senior post in the company's personnel division, and fell a few feet further when I revealed that I instead wanted a short-term secondment out of stores and into a job that involved "helping people". I didn't quite know what such a job might entail exactly, but I knew that M&S had a track record of supporting various good causes. Perhaps they could find me something along those lines?

I elaborated that whilst I was really enjoying my job with the company (a little white lie) I felt "called" to do something "a bit more altruistic" - and I had a feeling it would be good for me to "broaden my horizons". I also pointed out that this would be "great for the store", because they would be able to claim the secondment as a corporate social responsibility output and, furthermore, I would undoubtedly return with "renewed enthusiasm", which could only help me to become "an even better personnel manager".

It all made perfect sense, I thought. How could she refuse in the face of such well-reasoned and persuasive arguments? I had clearly demonstrated that *everyone* would come out of this a winner.

Her mouth smiled, but her voice was steely as she spoke. "I'm sorry, Brian, but that's quite out of the question. We're short-staffed in the division as it is, and we need all of our personnel managers in stores for the foreseeable future." Then, pulling a crisp twenty-pound note from her handbag and handing it to me, she continued, "Now be a dear and pop down to the sales floor and get me a ham sandwich and a new pair of 15 denier tights. I laddered mine on the wretched train."

With my escape route towards something that actually mattered to me so firmly closed off, it dawned on me in that moment that - if I *really* wanted to be happy - the only way was *out*. And happy was something I definitely wanted to be. I realised even then that I had to take matters into my own hands.

My first step was to start doing voluntary work in the sort of areas that interested me. I didn't have a Vital Vocation process to guide me back then, but I knew on some instinctive level that I *had* to make space in my life for the things that I most enjoyed doing – or nothing would ever change. I volunteered in a social work setting for a while and also gave some time to a voluntary buddying scheme which helped divert young offenders from future criminal activity.

The voluntary work was so successful and enjoyable, I was eventually offered a part-time job as a residential social worker in a care home for young people with challenging behaviours – in addition to my day job with M&S. I accepted the offer. It gave me a great opportunity to try out another line of work, and it fulfilled that part of me that just wasn't being fulfilled otherwise – but it was hard. My job at the store was very full-time, and doing this on top of it challenged me at every level.

On one occasion, after doing a long day's work as a personnel manager and then a hard day's night-shift at the care home, I fell asleep while getting a haircut. I think the barber was worried I'd expired on him. Clearly, something had to give, and I didn't want it to be my sanity.

I don't say this to impress you with my drive, determination or energy levels.

> *The important thing here is that I noticed what I felt called to do, and I took steps to do it. I understood even then that this would be the tactic that would help me find the golden thread to my ideal work.*

Which brings us back to that fateful day when I told my boss at the store that I wanted to resign. The relief I felt at finally admitting what had been bubbling up inside me for months was enormous. Fortunately for me, my boss was understanding and reassured me that she would provide a good reference and that I could take some time during my notice period to look for other work.

Propelled by the realization that I now had to *act* on my professional restlessness (or should that be "recklessness"?) I started looking around for other full-time jobs. In the meantime, my part-time social work job provided a useful buffer.

I found a new job pretty quickly (yes, times were different then). It meant taking a considerable pay cut – to almost half of my previous salary – and moving out of my spacious home into a much smaller pad. But it enabled me to take the leap from the commercial retail environment in which I had felt so stifled, to a fundraising position in a small charity that became an immediately comfortable fit. The drop in salary was a small price to pay for the privilege of working in an environment that enabled me to use my particular talents to their full effect.

In fact, my new job was a revelation. I was revitalized! My focus shifted from trying to maximise sales force productivity to helping impoverished people reduce their crippling debts. My productivity levels, and my enthusiasm, soared. It felt as if I had finally found my calling: a job that was based around my talents and values, and that left me feeling energized and alive rather than drained and dead. It felt like I had found my Vital Vocation. I have no doubt that I wouldn't have noticed the opportunity – much less been qualified for it – if I hadn't listened to that inner "pull" that guided me to do the voluntary work in social services.

Since that major career transition nearly twenty years ago, I've been through several further stages in refining my working life, and have developed an exciting portfolio career that remains a constant source of delight today. I'm now chief executive of a major local charity, I've built my own thriving coaching and consultancy practice and I've carved out a growing niche as a freelance writer. Professionally and personally speaking, I couldn't be happier – or more excited about the future.

Best of all, I've come to see that the career-design process I discovered (by accident and instinct as much as by intention) can be successfully applied by anyone, in any circumstance.

I will outline that process for you in this book, so you can apply it to *your* life.

I've coached and trained hundreds of people who were in the same place I was back then – tired, burned-out, disillusioned, fearful that things would never get better – and I'm yet to find a single one who hasn't been able to use the process I've designed to move towards their own Vital Vocation.

Whether you're in a dead-end job and longing for a change, long-term unemployed and losing hope, or just beginning to face the world of work full of fear and trepidation, this book is for you.

It's the book I wish I'd had at my side before I made that madcap decision to pack in my well-paid and secure job and take a leap into the unknown. It would have saved me many sleepless nights, I'm sure!

You'll be pleased to know that I'm not recommending that you do anything as drastic as throwing everything up in the air tomorrow and starting from scratch. All you need to do is read this book, diligently apply the step-by-step Vital Vocation process, and you'll be able to find or create the ideal work for you - and you can do it *without* giving up your current security.

In fact, the really good news is that you'll be able to do it from exactly where you are now, even if that means learning to love the job you're in, until you find a job you love.

Let's begin!

How to Use This Book

In my work as a career coach, I've noticed a couple of striking things in recent years.

Firstly, most of the clients who approach me with complaints of indefinable feelings of dissatisfaction are usually, upon closer investigation, deeply unhappy in their work.

Secondly, most of those clients either feel they don't *know* what career would make them truly happy or they *do* know, but don't believe they have a hope of getting it. I understand exactly where they're coming from, because I've been there too. But my own experience has taught me a really valuable lesson:

> *Sometimes, you just have to strike out in the vague direction of your dream, even if you don't know exactly where the journey's going to lead you. The very act of making the trip can reveal all the pieces that are missing.*

I've found that if I can help my clients identify some key pieces of information, and work with them to turn what they learn into a series of simple action steps, I can help set them on a path to the work they love.

In the course of developing a series of techniques to achieve this, the Vital Vocation process was born. I use it with my face-to-face coaching clients and I've also offered it as an online membership programme as well as in classroom training sessions.

Consequently, hundreds of people have now used this process and I'm pleased to say that the vast majority have gone on to find work they love (as well as a healthy balance between their work and home lives).

How This Book Can Help You

I've come to see that it's only possible to be truly happy and fulfilled if we're able to find and do the things we love to do on an (almost) daily basis. Who can be truly happy doing things they *don't* love to do?

So, my Vital Vocation process is firstly about finding the calling in our hearts and then listening to it very carefully so that we can hear what it has to tell us about what's going to make us really, truly happy.

You may be wondering if you even have a calling. Believe me, you do. We all do. It may be more of a whisper inside you than a roar, but it's there. It may even be that you've ignored it, because it's calling you to do something that some people (including you) would class as mundane, unimportant or unachievable. That doesn't matter. All that matters is that you find what *you* were designed to do, because doing what you were designed to do is the fast-track to your fulfilment.

I want to be very clear with you up front, however; this is not a "get any job at any cost" book and it's definitely not a "find an easy job that'll make you rich quick" book.

Your Vital Vocation might make you a fortune or it might make you next to nothing (except happy). I've discovered that the amount of money you make has very little to do with how fulfilling that work is going to be anyway, or how happy you'll end up in the long run. You do of course have to be able to make enough money to live, and everyone has a different definition of "enough".

So, if you were hoping for a get-rich-quick book, this isn't it, but it is one that can lead you to a life full of profound rewards.

There's something else you should know. The process I'm about to outline for you is a lot of fun, and very powerful, but it's also nuts-and-bolts practical. That's what makes it so effective. I'm not going to ask you to pump yourself full of positive thinking before you strike out in the direction of your Vital Vocation. Although we will be looking at how you can make your mind work for you, you'll find nothing in here about how to affirm your way to success, or cosmically-order the career of your dreams, or use the power of creative visualisation to turn yourself into a world-famous celebrity (unless that's what you really want to be of course, in which case you can use the Vital Vocation process for that, too). Instead, I'll be presenting you with a workable programme that you'll be able to apply whatever mood you happen to be in.

I'm also making no assumptions about what your Vital Vocation is going to look like. That's going to be your decision, no-one else's. I don't assume that you'll want to "escape the 9 to 5" (perhaps your Vital Vocation will turn out to be a very 9 to 5 kind of thing); but neither do I assume that you don't want to.

I don't pretend that there's a single "formula" that will unlock everyone's career puzzle. You won't have to set up a "niche website" if you don't want to, and I won't fool you into believing you should be aiming to make a fortune working for only a few hours a week out of a backpack in the Bahamas – again, unless that's what you *really* want to go for.

My only real interest is in helping you to attain deep satisfaction in your work and life, along with a feeling that at long last you can be yourself. If you can achieve that, you'll have achieved something that can't be priced.

The point of this book is to help you find whichever work/lifestyle model is right for you, and then to help you to make it a reality.

"Help! I've Just Lost My Job!"

If you've picked up this book because you've just lost your job – or you're scared that you might in the near future – then you must be feeling extremely anxious. This book doesn't focus on how you can keep the job you're in or how you can avoid being fired or made redundant in the future, but I'm well aware that many people are first impelled to look for their ideal profession precisely because they are faced with the real prospect of losing their current job.

If you're in that situation then before you go any further, I suggest you skip ahead and read my *Emergency Job-Loss Action Plan*, outlined in Chapter 9. That will help you take care of any immediate emergency issues and will help to calm your frazzled nerves. Once you've done that, you can come back here and start working your way through the rest of the book.

Why This Book Is Different

Many other career books do what our school careers advisers probably did: they help us to discover our skills and then tell us which jobs require those skills, so that we can go and get one of those jobs. I don't know about you, but I vividly remember filling in those career questionnaires that were then fed into a computer which chewed them up and spat out a long list of possible jobs (none of which seemed particularly appealing, mainly because I had very little idea of what most of them actually involved).

The Vital Vocation process is different, because finding our skills is one of the *last* things we'll be doing. I'll explain why in more detail later, but in short, it's because this book isn't just about finding work you'll be *able* to do; it's about finding work that you'll *love* to do.

Before we look at your skills, we'll uncover your gifts and talents (yes, you have them – several in fact) and we'll also investigate the values that you feel should underpin your life and work. These are the foundations upon which your Vital Vocation is going to be built.

The Shape of the Vital Vocation Process

The programme outlined in this book has been carefully designed to be completed sequentially; that is, you shouldn't attempt the work in any chapter until you've completed the material in the previous one.

> **Part 1 is all about *identifying* your Vital Vocation – or at least the outline of it – so that you're in a strong position to get it.** In many ways, this is the most important part of the book, because it covers the material that most people *don't* explore when they embark upon a job hunt or career change. Even if you know what your ideal work is, I encourage you to work through Part 1 anyway. I think you'll find it very enlightening and fun. There's nothing more exciting than self-discovery!

> **Part 2 is a bit shorter and is about *getting* your Vital Vocation; in other words, making it a reality in your life.** This book isn't primarily about job-hunting tips, interview techniques or learning how to write business plans, but Part 2 provides enough information about each of those things to get you started, and also directs you to a host of further resources. It will also help you to consider how to make the most of where you are now in your career, even if you're desperate to move on.

Throughout the book, each chapter gives you something to think about and you'll be asked to complete some easy, fun and very powerful written exercises that are designed to help you get the maximum possible insight from the material. Some chapters also have some powerful self-coaching questions; the kind of questions I might ask you if you were one of my coaching clients.

In the process of completing the exercises and answering the questions – many of which are specifically designed to challenge your usual way of thinking about the job-hunting process – the outline of your Vital Vocation will start to emerge.

How Long Does It Take?

You can work through the book at any pace you like, but I invite you to complete a maximum of one chapter a day, to allow yourself some space between each one. This will ensure that you have time to really think about each step as you complete the exercises. It will also give you enough time to let the learning from each chapter "sink in" before you move on.

Of course, you can choose to spend more than a day on each chapter if that works best for you. Similarly, if you're in a real hurry, you can move at a faster pace. You'll know what pace feels right.

Step-by-Step to the Work You Love

This is a practical, tactical, action-oriented programme. The old cliché holds true here; you'll get out of it what you put in. However, you may be surprised to find that the early exercises don't seem very practical at all. That's quite intentional. I actually don't want you to get too practical too soon. Here's why:

The problem most of us face when it comes to finding our ideal work is that we've closed our mind to the possibilities and have settled for doing the "right" or "practical" thing. You'll understand exactly what I mean if you've ever settled for a job that pays the bills but doesn't feed your spirit or leave you with enough free time to spend time on the things (and the people) that you love. This book is about taking a different approach.

> *The Vital Vocation process will help you to bust some of the myths that prevent you from unearthing your real gifts and talents.*

If we start off being too practical, we'll close off a whole range of interesting avenues that are genuinely worth exploring. You don't want that; you want to stretch your imagination so that all the relevant possibilities are up for grabs.

Later, we're going to get very practical indeed so that you will not only have identified your Vital Vocation, you'll also put together a step-by-step plan to help you get it.

I think you're going to be surprised to find that some of the options you used to think were impossibly out of reach are actually very attainable for you.

Getting Ready to Start

In order to get the most from this book, you're going to need to set aside some clearly defined space in three important areas:

1. **Your physical environment**. Make sure you're not distracted while you're going through the exercises. Being "tidy" means something different to each of us, so I'm not going to lecture you about making sure your desk is completely clean. But if you need to, take care of any outstanding business, clear away any annoying clutter, ask your family not to disturb you, and unplug the phone.

2. **Your calendar.** By purchasing this book, you've made an important investment in yourself. Make the most of it by committing to use it. Set aside a specific time for this work and write it in your calendar so that you don't forget. Ask your family and friends to respect your decision to take some time for yourself.

3. **Your mind.** Try to be as fresh as possible when you start working on your Vital Vocation exercises. If you can, allow extra time between working through the exercises and any other commitments you may have; do something relaxing beforehand or just go for a walk to clear your head. However, if time is tight, don't let that stop you. Just take a few deep, relaxing breaths before you begin to help you focus. Then get started.

EXERCISE 1: Your Vital Vocation Journal

Many of the exercises in the book are done by writing, so your first task is to prepare something to write in. You should do this in whatever way is easiest for you. You might want to do it on your computer, or you might want to do it with pen and paper. You may even want to do some of the exercises by recording your answers on a digital audio recorder (although not all of them are suited to this method).

I recommend that you buy yourself an exercise book (or create a file in your computer) and call it your Vital Vocation Journal. This will be the place where you complete most of your exercises, write the answers to the self-coaching questions and jot-down any thoughts, insights or ideas you have as you work through the book. As you can imagine, your journal will become an extremely valuable record of your journey.

If you're going to buy a book then treat yourself to the best you can afford, and some nice pens to go with it. What you'll be writing about is no less than your future, and that deserves your very best investment and attention.

I'm sure that you, like many of my clients, are going to look back at your Vital Vocation Journal with great interest once you've landed the job of your dreams.

PART ONE: FINDING IT

*An unfulfilled vocation drains the colour
from a man's entire existence.*

~ Honoré de Balzac

CHAPTER 1
WHAT IS A VITAL VOCATION?

If you follow your bliss you put yourself on a kind of track that has been there all the while, waiting for you, and the life that you ought to be living is the one you are living. Follow your bliss ... and doors will open where you didn't know they were going to be.

~ Joseph Campbell

Find out who you are and do it on purpose.

~ Dolly Parton

You're probably wondering about the title of this book. What *is* a Vital Vocation anyway? Let's break it down. This is what the Oxford English Dictionary has to say about the definition of *vocation*, a word that comes from the Latin verb *vocare* ("to call"):

vocation (noun)

- a strong feeling of suitability for a particular career or occupation

- a person's employment or main occupation, especially regarded as worthy and requiring dedication

- a trade or profession

And here's what it has to say about the definition of *vital*, a word derived from the Latin *vitalis,* which describes the animating principle of all living beings:

vital (adjective)

- *absolutely necessary; essential*
- *indispensable to the continuance of life*
- *full of energy; lively*

So, in short, a *Vital Vocation* describes a way of making a living which is in some way *essential* to your life, either because you feel a deep instinctive need for it or because it emerges naturally from your own unique way of being in the world. Put simply, it's a way of making a living that makes your heart and spirit sing!

A Vital Vocation is also "vital" to you because doing it enables you to feel alive and vibrant – full of the energy that a mediocre job just drains away.

There's *nothing* more exciting or fulfilling than doing work that enables you to be yourself. Many of us have had the experience of being stuck in jobs which do exactly the opposite; jobs that squeeze our personalities out of us and make us feel like lifeless, mindless drones. If you've been in that position in the past, or are in it now, you'll understand just how important it is to make a change. That's why I created the Vital Vocation process for my clients.

Why You Should Find Your Vital Vocation

Think it's too frivolous and maybe even a bit selfish to go off in search of the work you love? Think again. The world needs *more* people who are following their calling and sharing their gifts with the rest of humanity, not fewer.

A few years ago, Bonnie Ware, a nurse who worked for many years in palliative care, published a list of the top five regrets people express on their deathbeds (http://www.inspirationandchai.com/Regrets-of-the-Dying.html). She found that the number one regret expressed by the dying was:

"I wish I'd had the courage to live a life true to myself, not the life others expected of me."

A sobering thought. As Oliver Wendell Holmes wrote so movingly in his poem *The Voiceless* in 1858: "Alas for those that never sing, but die with all their music in them!"

Don't be one of them. Share what you have with the rest of us. For better or worse, you've been given the gift of life, and answering your calling is the gift you can give back in return.

The Two Paths to a Vital Vocation

I have some good news for you. There are not one but *two* basic paths to your Vital Vocation:

> The first is to find your **ideal job**, one which uses one or more of your main gifts and talents in a deeply fulfilling and financially rewarding way.

> The second is to find a **good-enough job**, which uses one or more of your ancillary skills, pays the bills, doesn't cause you too much stress, and leaves you with enough time to pursue your real passions outside of work time.

The reason that's such good news is because it means that finding your Vital Vocation *isn't* always about finding the 'perfect job'. That takes some of the pressure off because it gives you scope to make a living in a variety of ways, whilst ensuring that you include time in your life for your passions – either on the job or off it.

Bear in mind that in either case, your Vital Vocation may consist of more than one activity that generates income for you. In fact, having several income streams can be a great way of adding flexibility to your life, particularly if you have a range of interests.

One of my clients – Andy - now works part-time as a teacher (a job he adores) so that he can help his partner with their business, an antiques shop (which he also adores). His Vital Vocation is to do *both* of these things, and the two income streams certainly don't hurt.

Mary retired early from a job that didn't make her happy – and now works as a cleaner to make just enough money to supplement her pension. This supports her and leaves her with enough free time to pursue her real love, which is to create art; beautiful paintings that she's just beginning to build up the courage to offer for sale. Although it's little more than a hobby at the moment, I suspect that this will become another income stream for her in the future – and quite possibly a burgeoning career.

The point is, there isn't a single "right" way to make your Vital Vocation a reality in your life. The only "right" way is the one that works for you. Of course, an important starting point is to discover what your passions actually are, if you don't already know. That's one of things we'll be doing shortly, so don't be too concerned if you're thinking, "But I don't know what I'm passionate about!"

You may also believe that building a life around your passions is impossible. Again, don't worry; that's just one of the myths we'll be dismantling soon.

Taking a Closer Look: The Four Essential Factors of Your Vital Vocation

Everyone's Vital Vocation is made up of four essential factors. By identifying what form these factors need to take for *you* to feel content, you can begin to identify the details of your own Vital Vocation – the work that will make you happiest. As you fill in the details of each factor, then bit by bit, the outline of your Vital Vocation will emerge like the details of a developing photograph.

Factor 1: TALENTS	Factor 2: VALUES
• Explicit • Implicit	• What matters most to you • The needs you see in the world
Factor 3: ENVIRONMENT	Factor 4: SKILLS
• People • Place • Workplace type • Reward level	• Functional • Intellectual

Let's take a closer look at each factor and the important elements within it:

Factor 1: Talents

Talents are your **natural aptitudes**: the things you're inherently good at. They can either be:

> **Explicit talents**, which you (and the people around you) *know* you're good at. These talents are obvious both to you and to the rest of the world.

> **Implicit talents,** which are the hidden gifts you may have to do some digging to find. These are talents that others recognise in you before you recognise them yourself. They may even be gifts no one, including yourself, even realises you possess *until you go looking for them.*

Factor 2: Values

Values are those **principles and standards of behaviour** which are deeply important to you and which are derived from your own particular personality and view of the world. They can be broken down into:

> **The things that matter most to you**: those behaviours and beliefs you *need to express in order to feel wholly yourself.* These might include your political or religious convictions.

> **The needs you see in the world**: those conditions you regard as a "call to action". They might include your *drive to help others* through charity or through channelling your time and influence in particular directions.

Factor 3: Environment

Environment is the **physical, social and psychological place** you want to be in as you carry out your work. There are a number of important elements here:

> **The people** you want to work with, for and on behalf of, including colleagues, customers, supervisors, subordinates and associates.

> **The location** in the world where you want to work and live. This includes details such as continent, country, state, town, street and whether you work indoors in an office or outdoors in an orchard.

> **The type of work environment** you need in order to thrive. A busy one or one that's slow-moving? Is it supportive or constantly challenging? Do you prefer something that's traditional or modern?

> **The reward level** you need in order to live a comfortable and balanced life. Details to consider here include salary, the costs of working in this particular situation and any added perks of the job.

Factor 4: Skills

Skills are the **abilities you've developed over time** and learned to carry out competently. These can either be:

> **Functional skills**, which are those things you can *do* well. They are generally actions: typing, knitting, driving, writing computer software, deep-sea diving…

> **Intellectual skills**, which are those things you *know* a lot about. They are generally areas of expertise: the works of Shakespeare, history, the French language, horticulture, astrophysics, nutrition, the Renaissance…

Of course, some skills can fit into both categories, because they require you to *know* a lot about the things you're *doing* – like brain surgery. At least, I hope that's the case when it comes to brain surgery...

Over the course of the following chapters, we'll be looking in detail at each of these four factors and the elements that underlie them.

By deeply examining each factor we'll be able to build up a detailed picture of your Vital Vocation. We may not come up with a picture of a specific job for you to apply for (although that certainly could happen) but we'll have a very clear template which can be used to help you find (or create) the right work for you, whether that's as an employee, a self-employed person or freelancer, or even as a business owner.

Your Talents are the Key to Your Contentment

The factors above are listed in order of importance (talents, values, environment, skills).

We always begin the process by identifying and exploring our talents and we'll go into this in much more detail in Chapter 2. This is because your ideal work will either be built around your talents or will be work that frees you up to use your talents in your free time.

> *Remember: finding your talents is the key to unlocking your Vital Vocation.*

As I mentioned earlier, you've probably been taught – or read other careers advice books that teach – that *skills* are the most important thing to consider in your career search. However, although they are undoubtedly important, the skills you need can be learned, whereas talents are innate.

It's also worth remembering that you'll have lots of skills which you may *not* want to use in your career. I'm very skilled at cleaning my kitchen cupboards, but it's not something I want to do for a living (there are other people who do it far better). If you build your career search around your skills, you may find your way into work that you're very good at, but which you don't particularly enjoy. This can result in a classic case of, "I got to the top of the career ladder – only to discover that it was leaning against the wrong wall!"

You can be sure, however, that your talents and what you love doing are *always* intimately connected. That's why we'll begin this process by doing something that's incredibly useful and also a *lot* of fun – going in search of the things you love the most in this life.

 EXERCISE 2: First Impressions

Turn to a clean page in your Vital Vocation Journal. At the top of it, write *My Vital Vocation – First Impressions.*

Without thinking about it too deeply, take five minutes to jot down which *talents, values, environmental factors* and *skills* spring to mind when you ask yourself the question, "What is my Vital Vocation going to look like?"

Don't spend too long on this. It isn't a trick question; it's just designed to help you get down on paper whatever thoughts you're already having about your ideal work.

We'll come back to what you've written later. It'll be interesting to compare what you write here with what you learn as you move through the book.

Self-Coaching Questions

Take your time, think deeply and record the answers in your journal.

1. What do you know already about what you were born to do?

2. Name three specific things that would definitely be part of your ideal career - and three things that definitely wouldn't.

3. What have you done in your life that has been the most successful, or most beneficial to other people?

CHAPTER 2
TALENTS

What you love is what you are gifted at, and there are no exceptions.

~ Barbara Sher

This chapter is action-orientated and is all about finding the key that unlocks your Vital Vocation. It's where we go in search of your gifts and talents in the sure knowledge that these lie at the root of your ideal work. If you already think you know what they are, great; now's your chance to verify that. If you don't, the exercises in this chapter will really help you to unearth them.

Discovering What Makes You Tick

The simplest way to get a hint of where your talents lie is to pay attention to anything that you are attracted to and in particular, anything that you really *love*.

Even if you don't have an obvious talent in that area, you can be sure that your love for a thing points you towards a talent of some sort. Perhaps it will be something as simple as the fact that you have a heightened appreciation of the subject in question. Yes, that *is* a real talent. An expert wine-taster doesn't need to be able to make wine, but he or she needs to fully appreciate good wine in order to do the job well. A history teacher may never make history, but he or she needs to love learning about it in order to teach it effectively. So it is with you. If you love something, you see it in a particular way: a way that's utterly unique and therefore very valuable to you, and to others.

In order to cast the net as wide as possible, I'm going to ask you to explore several areas which will provide you with clues as to what you should be doing with your life. In the exercises that follow we'll be searching for this treasure in:

- **Your memories**
- **Your future plans**
- **Your imagination**
- **Other people's perceptions of you**
- **Your unconscious mind**

Each area is explored in a separate exercise and I'll give examples from my own life so that you can see how it's done.

It's worth giving yourself sufficient time to do each exercise without having to rush through it. By going searching for what you love in each of these areas (the last two are optional) you'll be able to gather enough information to spot any pattern in the things that are capable of satisfying and stimulating you. Once you can see a pattern like that, you can begin to build a life and career around it.

Ready? Enjoy this. We're about to do no less than discover your purpose in life!

 EXERCISE 3: Journeying into the Past

For this exercise, you're going to cast your mind back to things you've loved doing in your past.

Step 1

Wherever you are just now in your life, think back to several earlier periods, for example:

- **Childhood**
- **Your teenage years**
- **Young adulthood**
- **Adulthood**
- **Middle age**

Write each of the periods you've chosen as a heading on a separate page and make a list of all the things you *really loved to do* when you were that age. List as many as you can recall and be as specific as possible.

However – and this is important – *only* write down the things you particularly loved. Choose things that would rate a 7 or above if you were to rate them on a "lovability scale" of 1 to 10 (with 10 being highest).

Don't censor yourself. Everything is relevant here, so add anything you think of to the list, even if it seems unimportant or ridiculous (believe me: it isn't, as long as it scores above 7 on your "lovability" scale).

Here's what my list might look like:

Childhood:

Playing in my sandpit and making up stories to go with the buildings I was making out of sand; pretending to be a superhero, especially one with magical powers; reading comics; riding my bike; making up stories and illustrating them on my blackboard; dancing to loud music on Top of the Pops; *watching old films; anything to do with witches, especially* The Wizard of Oz; *watching* Doctor Who *and never missing* Wonder Woman *on television; watching my grandmother baking.*

Teenage Years:

Reading books, especially fantasy and science fiction; writing my own short stories, usually about supernatural subjects; drawing, particularly faces; listening to pop music and imagining that I might be a pop star one day; hanging around with my friends and making them laugh.

Young Adulthood:

Entering short story competitions; going out with friends to clubs with good dance music; volunteering for charitable organisations, particularly those working with disadvantaged groups and young people; studying Shakespeare, particularly the tragedies and romances; practising yoga; cooking, particularly healthy foods.

Step 2

Next, trawl through your list and make a note of what you loved most about all the things you've listed, even if they aren't things you'd necessarily enjoy doing now.

What you're doing here is analysing what it was about those activities that attracted you. Instead of dismissing them out of hand or saying, "I've grown out of that now," you're re-looking at them with the curiosity of a scholar. You might be surprised at what you find.

My analysed list might look partially like this:

Childhood:

Playing in my sandpit and making up stories to go with the buildings I was making out of sand.
I loved being creative, and being responsible for building something that hadn't existed before I brought it into the world.

Playing at being a superhero, especially one with magical powers.
I loved the idea of being able help people in need and I loved the excitement of the idea that with magical powers, you could do anything you wanted.

Dancing to loud music on *Top of the Pops*.
I loved the sense of freedom and moving my body to the rhythm of the music.

Anything to do with witches, especially *The Wizard of Oz*.
I was fascinated by the Wicked Witch and the fact that she could fly on a broomstick and had an army of magic monkeys.

Teenager:

Reading books, especially fantasy and science fiction.
I loved losing myself in magical worlds and admiring the skill of the writers who were able to make those worlds believable.

Writing my own short stories, usually about supernatural subjects.
I loved being creative, using words to evoke emotions in other people and exploring magical themes with my imagination.

Listening to pop music and imagining that I might be a pop star one day.
I loved the glamour of pop music, the life-affirming sound of the music and the idea of entertaining people and having them want to listen to me.

Young Adulthood:

Entering short story competitions.
I loved the challenge of competing and the sense of accomplishment when I won a competition and had a story

published.

Volunteering for charitable organisations, particularly those who work with disadvantaged groups and young people.
I loved using my spare time to help other people, whilst learning new skills.

Practising yoga.
I loved developing my flexibility and fitness.

Step 3

Now it's time to look for what I call "threads and themes" – recurring patterns in the activities you loved and the things you loved most about them. Go through your analysed list from Step 2 and make a note of any themes and patterns you notice.

Here are some of the threads and themes I might come up with from my list:

- **Being creative and stretching my imagination**
- **Helping others**
- **Entertaining people and making them laugh**
- **Learning new things and stretching myself**
- **Writing and having others appreciate my writing**
- **Experiencing a sense of physical strength, flexibility and freedom**

Got the idea? Take some time over this. It should take you at least 30 minutes to do this properly – probably longer. Don't short change yourself. You're doing nothing less than beginning to sketch out the criteria that you'll need to satisfy in order to live a life of pleasure, meaning and purpose.

EXERCISE 4: Careering into the Future

For this exercise, you're going to project your mind forward into careers you've thought about doing in the future – even things that you've considered and rejected.

When I was very young – four or five – I proudly announced to my parents that I wanted to be a pilot. I was terribly excited by this prospect and absolutely sure that this was what I was going to be when I grew up. The only problem was that I didn't actually know what a pilot was. When my dad happened to mention that pilots were very clever people to be able fly aeroplanes, I was horrified and promptly decided a pilot's life wasn't for me.

Step 1

Make a list of everything you've ever considered doing for a living "in the future".

Leave nothing out – even the most outlandish ideas. The only things not to include are things other people told you that you "should" or "could" do. We want only the things that appealed to *you* at some stage, even if you later changed your mind and rejected them.

My list might look like this:

- Pilot
- Chef
- Teacher
- Astronaut
- Vet
- Pop Star

- Priest
- Lawyer
- Author

Step 2

Next, go through your list and make a note of *why* you wanted to do that job and – for all those you didn't ultimately become – *why* you didn't.

My analysed list might look partially like this:

Pilot: *I just loved the sound of the word! It was mysterious and powerful, and it sounded like someone who was very sure of who and what they were. I rejected this idea when I discovered that pilots actually had to go up in the air and fly aeroplanes. No thanks!*

Chef: *I've always loved cooking and really loved the idea of being able to create my own recipes and sharing them with others. I rejected the idea because I didn't like the idea of having to cook under pressure to tight timescales, in baking hot kitchens, to other people's instructions!*

Teacher: *My parents were teachers, so I had some idea of what this involved – good and bad. It attracted me because I've always enjoyed sharing useful ideas with other people and in particular, finding ways of making complicated information simple and accessible. I eventually rejected the idea because I knew that I wouldn't enjoy trying to teach people who didn't want to learn, and also because I didn't want to have to undertake this particular type of training. However, I always thought this was something I might come back to in some form in the future.*

Pop Star: *I liked the idea of the glamour and of being able to entertain people and make them happy by performing for* *them on stage. I rejected this idea because I can't sing!*

Astronaut: *As a child, I was fascinated by science fiction stories, especially those in comic strips like* Dan Dare *and* Judge Dredd. *I rejected this because I knew that, whilst I enjoyed travelling in space in my imagination, to do it in reality would take too great an investment of time and energy.*

Lawyer: *This one really shouldn't be on the list. This wasn't ever a serious consideration for me, although some friends and relatives did tell me they thought I'd make a good lawyer because they could see I enjoyed a good debate (I think they meant I was argumentative). It never really appealed to me because it felt too "fact-based" without room for creativity (I'm sure many lawyers would disagree, but that's how I saw it then).*

Author: *This appealed because I've always loved writing and I've always got pleasure from knowing that others have enjoyed my writing. I've never really rejected this idea and it's still very much part of my life and my plans.*

Step 3

It's "threads and themes" time again.

First, make a list of the obvious things that spring out to you as being themes in the things you liked about your imagined future careers. Let's call this "List A". Here are some of the threads and themes I might come up with for my list:

- **Conveying information to others**
- **Helping others with my writing and communication**
- **Performing in front of people**
- **Being creative and sharing my creativity with others**

Next, go through the reasons why you *rejected* those careers and make a note of the things that turned you off about them. This is "List B". Here's what my List B might look like:

- **Working in a hot, fast, pressurised environment**
- **Working with machinery I'm not very interested in**
- **Trying to communicate with a reluctant audience**
- **Having my creativity stifled or curtailed**

Finally, make another list by turning the reasons you rejected those careers into "opposite statements" which describe the criteria of careers you *would* consider. We'll call this "List C". For example, I'd take the list above and turn it around to:

- **Working in a steady environment where I was able to feel calm and in control**
- **Working with materials that interest and excite me, probably words, information or plant-based materials**
- **Communicating with a lively, eager, engaged audience**
- **Being able to fully express my creativity**

Now, put "List A" and "List C" together into a single list, which we'll call "List D". .Again, this exercise should take at least 30 minutes to do. At the end of it, List D will be a list of the criteria that were important to you when you seriously considered career options, and which may well *still* be important to you now.

You may be noticing some similarities between what you found in Exercise 3 and this exercise; or you may find that some new themes have emerged. Either outcome is fine. We'll be coming back later to examine everything we're discovering here.

Don't look now, but your dreams and wishes are beginning to emerge from the shadows!

✏ EXERCISE 5: Wearing New Hats

Have you ever wished you could be someone else for a day, like Mr. Benn in the old cartoon? Well, now you can – several people, in fact. This exercise is about using your imagination to try on some new hats, so they can tell you something about what it would take for you to build a life and career you'll love.

Step 1

Pick six or seven real people – you don't have to know them personally – who you'd like to be for a day. Try to pick five or six diverse people. They don't all have to be specific names; they can be generic categories of people like "a bus conductor" or "a scientist". They also don't have to be the same sex as you. In fact, try to ensure you include *at least* one person of the opposite sex in your list.

Remember, you've got the opportunity here to try out being someone completely different. Make the most of it. The only proviso is that you shouldn't pick anyone you feel no desire to spend a day being. You've got to feel some genuine attraction to living a day of this person's life. Remember your "lovability" scale of zero to ten and go for people whose lives seem to you to be a 7 or above.

My list might look like this:

- Joseph Campbell (the famous professor of mythology)
- William Shakespeare
- Dolly Parton
- A psychology lecturer
- Stan Lee (creator and writer of the *Spider Man* comic strip)

- An art teacher
- An ethno botanist

Step 2

For each person, write an outline of their ideal day as you conceive it to be. You might want to write it out in diary format. Do this for each of the people you selected. Make sure you pick an *ideal* day: a day in which they (you) do your favourite things, in your favourite type of environment with your favourite kinds of people.

Here's what two of my ideal days might look like (you should make yours even more detailed than this):

Joseph Campbell

AM – Woke up at sunrise and went for a walk on the beach in front of my house in Hawaii, listening to the waves lap on the sand, and contemplating the importance of symbols in human culture.

PM – Led a workshop on The Hero's Journey in World Mythology with a group of eager and lively students. We spent a considerable amount of time discussing the importance of finding your life's purpose by "following your bliss" – that activity which causes you to lose all sense of time and constraint.

Evening – After dining with my wife and discussing our respective days, spent an hour or so working on a book I'm editing on the collected writings of Carl Jung, then had an early night.

Dolly Parton

AM – I'm on tour, so I got up a bit later than usual and after meditating and praying, I spent an hour or so working on some new songs, which I'm planning on putting on my next album. My husband is accompanying me on this tour, so we had a late breakfast together before he went into town to catch up with some friends, and I finished off a couple more songs.

PM – I met an old friend for lunch and we caught up on old times then I went to the local branch of the publishing company I own and spent a couple of hours in an office they had prepared for me, taking care of business. I'm planning a new revue at Dollywood – the amusement park I own in the foothills of East Tennessee – and I'm also working on launching another European chapter of my Imagination Library, which gives free books to pre-school-age children from poor families. Then I returned to my hotel to get some rest before the show.

Evening – The show went really well; the crowd were very friendly and lively, and I felt I gave a great performance. Two encores! No show tomorrow and I even have enough time before we move on to the next date to explore the city, so spent some time planning that before bed.

Now, follow that process for all of your chosen people. Make sure you make their itineraries as detailed and varied as possible. Here's where you can really let your imagination run wild.

Don't worry about being realistic. Of course I don't know exactly what a day in Dolly Parton's life looks like, but I can imagine what I'd spend my time doing if *I* were Dolly. The more detailed you get, the more material you'll have to work with in Step 3.

Step 3

Threads and themes…

First, make a note of any themes you notice across all (or most) of your chosen lives. In my example above, the themes of performing, teaching, studying, owning my own business and interacting with others all stand out to me. What themes stand out for you in what you've written?

Then, make a note of the things that seem to you to be *absolutely essential* in an "ideal day". Think carefully here. If you could have only a few elements from each of these fantasies in your real life right now, what would they be?

In my case, I might write: *expressing my creativity; engaging in lively discussions; spending time with people I care about and respect; spending some time in quiet contemplation; having a variety of tasks to undertake so I'm never bored.*

Give yourself plenty of time for this exercise; you're going to be doing lots of imagining, lots of writing and lots of analysing. This could take at least an hour. Yes, it's a lot of work, but it's worth it.

Remember this: our lives are shaped by the things we do on a daily basis and you've just taken the first steps towards understanding what elements you need to include in your daily life if you're going to feel contented and purposeful.

A Pause for Thought...

The three exercises you've just done are pretty powerful. I've had clients and workshop participants report to me that they've been amazed at what they've discovered, just by following the steps in these exercises, and then looking for the "threads and themes" that ran through their answers.

You may want to take some time at this point to take stock of what you've learned. Are you finding that you knew more than you thought you did about the things you love to do? Is your purpose in life becoming just a *little* bit less murky?

If you had any doubts previously, I hope your belief is growing that it *is* possible for you to find something meaningful to do with your life. To help you along, take a moment or two to think about the answers to the following self-coaching questions, based on the "threads and themes" you've identified in the previous exercises.

Don't over-analyse, or spend too long on these. They're just intended to prompt you, not tax you, and there are no right or wrong answers. Jot down your impressions in your Journal as you read the questions.

 ## Self-Coaching Questions

1. What have you learned so far about the things that interest and inspire you?

2. What kinds of people have you felt most drawn to throughout your life?

3. What do the threads and themes you identified tell you about the kind of environments you feel most comfortable in?

4. Based on the answers to the exercises, what stands out to you about the contribution you'd like to make to the world? What would you like to change or improve?

5. What beliefs do your favourite activities appear to express? Do you value scientific endeavours more than artistic? Is it more important to work with people, information or objects?

6. What would you do if you were not limited by time or money? If you didn't have to choose a limited number of things to focus on, what are the things you'd like to include in an ideal life?

7. What would you like to be acknowledged for? In the exercises above, did you discover that the responses of other people were in any way important to you? If so, in what way?

Going Deeper

The search for a life-style involves a journey to the interior. This is not altogether a pleasant experience, because you not only have to take stock of what you consider your assets but also have to take a long look at what your friends call "the trouble with you". Nevertheless, the journey is worth making. Indeed, we might say that the whole purpose of existence is to reconcile the glowing opinion we have of ourselves with the terrible things other people say about us.

~ Quentin Crisp

The next two exercises are designed to enable you to look at the question of your life and work purpose from two very distinct perspectives.

I don't recommend that you undertake these exercises without having completed the previous three exercises first. In fact, consider the next two exercises as "optional extras" – not essential, but very revealing. If you don't want to do these, just move straight to Exercise 8.

The first exercise looks at the perceptions that other people have of us. This is always a tricky area, of course, and I'm certainly not suggesting that you build a life around what other people think you should be doing! However, it is useful to find out from others what they see as being your unique talents, abilities and interests. This can be revealing and instructive, and will often provide insights into your talents that you'd never have found on your own – but you've got to pick the right people. No critics allowed, not at this stage. You'll need to think of some trusted contacts for this exercise, so that you can get the full benefit of seeing yourself through someone else's eyes.

The second exercise gives you an opportunity to tap into a part of yourself that you may not be familiar with – not in your daily waking life, that is. We'll be using a technique which will enable you to turn down the volume on your "inner critic" – that internal voice that keeps telling you what you *can't* do, rather than what you *can* do – so that you can explore some options from a level of your perception that's somewhat deeper than your normal, conscious, waking state.

Don't worry if you don't feel willing or able at this stage to undertake these exercises. They are more intense than the previous three, so if you'd rather leave them for now, that's fine. These exercises will still be there, ready and waiting for you, when you're ready.

 EXERCISE 6: Crowdsourcing

O wad some Pow'r the giftie gie us
To see oursels as ithers see us!

~ Robert Burns, *To A Louse*

It seems to be a fact of human nature that we often have better ideas about what's best for other people than we do about what's best for ourselves. Perhaps that's because, with a bit of distance, it's easier to get perspective. Whatever the psychology behind it, we're going to make use of that principle to encourage a few more of your gifts out of the shadows.

Step 1

Think of all the times you've heard anyone comment or compliment you on the things you've done really well, and which you enjoyed but which felt fairly effortless to you. Family, friends, co-workers, acquaintances, strangers – anyone. Again, don't focus on your skills. We're not interested in the things you've done competently but don't love (they have their place, but it isn't in this exercise).

Think specifically about the times that someone has pointed out to you that you're *really good* at something – particularly those occasions when they noticed something that you didn't, because to you it was a perfectly natural thing for you to be doing.

Take your time and make a list. Get as much information as you can from your memories. Don't worry if you don't feel that it's very much, because the next stage is to actually ask others directly.

My list might look like this:

- **"You're a very good listener"**
- **"You're very patient when you're explaining something to someone"**
- **"You've got a way with words"**

Step 2

For this part of the exercise, you need to find at least one person that you trust to give you an honest – and kind – opinion. In choosing someone (you can choose more than one person) think carefully. No Pollyanna-ish, ultra-positive folks who'll just say what they think you want to hear; and no hyper-critical people who take pleasure in putting you down.

That's important, because you're going to ask them to give you their opinion of what you're good at. Not what you "should" be good at, based on your skills, or the job market, or their opinion or what your parents or neighbours will say, but rather what they think you're *actually good at*, based on their observations of your talents and passions.

Once you've got that from them, make sure you note it down.

If you're asking more than one person, note their answers too and add them to the list you created in Step 1.

My additions to the list might look like this:

- **"You're very easy to talk to"**
- **"You're very diplomatic, even when things get heated"**
- **"You're able to inject humour into otherwise boring situations"**

Step 3

By now, you know the drill! Take a good look at your list and extract the threads and themes you see. You should have a growing list of threads and themes (or it may be quite a short list, which is being reconfirmed by each new exercise – either is fine).

 EXERCISE 7: Into the Unconscious

This final exercise is purely and simply a method of allowing your imagination to flow freely without the fetters of the "inner critic" – that internal, nay-saying voice that tells you why a dream is impossible, even as it arises in your mind and heart.

So far, I've encouraged you to not get too practical and to allow your imagination to run freely. However, it's very difficult to turn our inner critic off completely, so just in case you have censored yourself – perhaps without even being aware of it – I invite you to try this exercise.

Be warned: it's not for the faint-hearted because it's so powerful, but it is actually very simple to do.

Step 1

For a week, or as many days as you can manage, set your alarm for half an hour earlier than normal. You'll need to place a notepad and pen beside your bed before you go to sleep. You could use your Vital Vocation Journal for this.

Step 2

The moment you awake in the morning, and without talking to anyone or reading anything, *immediately pick up your pad and pen and begin to write about any of the following topics* (it's best to decide which one the night before):

- **Things you loved to do as a child, toddler, teenager or young adult**
- **Your daydreams and ambitions for the future**
- **The ideal day of another person whose life is attractive to you**

You will realise of course that the topics are the same as those we covered in the previous exercises. In effect, you are doing the first part of those exercises while your brain is still in the relaxed space between sleep and full wakefulness.

Write for a full 30 minutes then put your pad aside without reading what you've written. Yes, you'll be half asleep as you do it – that doesn't matter. In fact, that's the whole point. As drowsy and dopey as you probably feel, just start writing and 30 minutes later, stop.

Step 3

Repeat this process each day (without reading what you wrote the day before). Once you've got to the end of the week – or have at least completed several days of writing – read what you've written and look for some threads and themes, just as you've been doing throughout these exercises.

It may seem like a strange and frivolous activity to undertake, but I think you'll be surprised at what it reveals to you.

I first used this method after reading about it in Dorothea Brande's wonderful book *Becoming a Writer*. I wasn't on a quest to find my life's purpose, but I was looking for ways to improve my writing skills. For a little short of two weeks, I woke every morning, half an hour earlier than usual, and began writing about anything that popped into my head. The exercise forbade me from reading what I had written until the two-week period was up, because the idea there – as here – was to allow creativity to flow freely and unfettered, straight from the unconscious.

When I eventually looked at what I had written, I was very surprised at what I had come up with. Not only was it far more imaginative than I expected, it was also far better written! It's a fun technique – and very instructive – although it's one that requires some discipline and a little bit of lost sleep.

Putting it Together: A Final Task

Take a deep breath – you're on the homeward straight. By now, you should have an impressive list of things you've loved in the past, in your imagination and in your planned future. In addition, you should have a number of things on the list that seem "new" to you; perhaps they are things you thought of doing at some point and dismissed, or perhaps they are even things you'd never have thought of before, but now realise they hold some fascination for you.

You should also have a list of some significant "threads and themes" that run through most, if not all, of the things you've discovered. Let's pull that information together.

✏️ VITAL VOCATION ROUND-UP 1: Talents

Step 1

Revisit the questions in Exercise 2: First Impressions, reconsidering them in the light of your now-expanded list. Has anything changed? Do you have anything to add to your impressions?

Go through your list of threads and themes, and look for threads and themes *within that list*. What *really* stands out to you now? Use this information to write yourself a Talents Statement – a short paragraph that encapsulates what you've discovered about *your* talents.

When I did this, based on the personal examples I've been using throughout this chapter, I wrote the following Talents Statement:

"I notice the recurring themes of teaching, communicating, writing and performing for the pleasure of others and myself. I also seem to like the idea of being in charge of my own work, perhaps owning my own business, and certainly being able to express my creativity in ways that are fun to me and hopefully of help to others."

I think that gives a pretty good summation of what I've come to believe is my purpose in life, and of what I've been building my lifestyle and career choices around for some time now. I'm able to utilise these talents in my career as a writer, coach, and charity chief executive.

What patterns do you notice in *your* threads and themes, and what does that pattern tell you about the purpose of *your* life? What gifts and talents have you discovered?

Step 2

Take a clean page in your journal and give it the title "Talents". Write the list of your key talents on this page, along with your Talents Statement and any other impressions you've received about your own unique gifts.

Well done! You've been on an intense journey in this chapter. You may have made some interesting discoveries, but you may also be feeling that you're still not quite sure of what you're going to be doing with the rest of your life or career. That's fine. Remember: your gifts and talents, though pivotally important, are only *one* part of what goes into making your Vital Vocation. The next important question for you to ask yourself is, "What matters most to me?"

Let's find out...

CHAPTER 3
VALUES

You get much more than a paycheck from your work.
If most of your important values are rewarded, you're
well on the way to a very satisfying life.

~ Nicholas Lore

People are pulled by values.

~ Viktor E. Frankl

What Do You Value?

We've taken a close look at your personal profile of talents. The question now is: what do you want to *do* with those talents? What principles and standards do you want your life to serve, and how will you express these principles through your work?

The talents you were born with can be made to serve almost any purpose you choose. To feel fulfilled, however, you must be clear about how you want to put them to use. It's an essential part of building a career – and a life – that you love.

What are Values, Anyway?

Put simply, values are the principles and standards that are, to you, intrinsically desirable, worthwhile and important. Whether we're conscious of it or not, each of us develops a unique system of values that determines how we feel about a whole range of things in life, including our family, our finances, our personal relationships and, of course, our work.

Values are complex constructs built on a combination of our views of acceptable principles and standards of behaviour (our own and other people's) along with our opinions about what is most important in life (e.g. "money" or "love" or "kindness"). Values can also relate to the needs we see in the world - the aspects of the world around us that we feel need to be supported or changed for the better. Consequently, values can help pull us towards a particular goal or lifestyle.

Although morality can have an influence on the creation of our values – particularly if we are strongly guided by a particular code of conduct determined by our political or religious persuasion – it's important to realise that there are no such things as *absolute values* in reality, because values differ across cultures, societies and individuals.

For the purpose of discovering your Vital Vocation, the most important thing is to make a choice about what is important to you, not what you think *should* be important to you based on the opinions of another person, doctrine or even a whole society. We'll begin by looking at what you already know about your values.

 EXERCISE 8: Finding Your Own Life Values

Step 1

Set a clock timer for five minutes. As soon as it's counting down, read through the following list of possible values and jot down *only* those that immediately stand out to you as being vitally important. If they don't seem essential to you, don't jot them down. If you can think of any essential values that are important to you that are not on the list, write them down too. Do this before reading any further.

- Achievement
- Adventure
- Affection
- Appearance
- Art
- Autonomy
- Belonging
- Building
- Challenge
- Children
- Competition
- Connection
- Contribution
- Control
- Cooperation
- Courage
- Creativity
- Dignity
- Empowerment
- Enlightenment
- Entrepreneurship
- Equality
- Esteem
- Excellence
- Expression
- Fame
- Family
- Financial security
- Freedom
- Friendship
- Fulfilment
- Giving
- Goodness
- Happiness
- Hard work
- Harmony
- Health
- Honesty
- Humour
- Independence
- Individuality
- Innovation
- Integrity
- Invention
- Justice
- Leadership
- Learning
- Leisure
- Looking good
- Love
- Loyalty
- Making money
- Marriage
- Mastery
- Order
- Peace
- Perseverance
- Personal development
- Play
- Privacy
- Progression
- Quality
- Recognition
- Reliability
- Religion
- Respect
- Revolution
- Safety
- Security
- Self-control
- Self-esteem
- Self-expression
- Service
- Sexuality
- Simplicity
- Socialising
- Spirituality
- Spontaneity
- Strength
- Synergy
- Trust
- Uniqueness
- Wealth
- Wisdom
- Youth

Step 2

Have a go at prioritising your list. You can either do that by instinct or you could use an online prioritising matrix. There's one at www.prioritizer.idea-sandbox.com or you can Google for one.

Step 3

Write "clarifying statements" for each of your top ten or fifteen values. See below for an example from Benjamin Franklin.

Benjamin Franklin's Virtues

Reading Benjamin Franklin's biography could leave you with a bit of an inferiority complex. Franklin was one of the founding fathers of the United States. A polymath, he was a leading author, printer, political theorist, politician, postmaster, scientist, musician, inventor, satirist, activist, statesman and diplomat. He played a major part in the American Enlightenment and in the history of physics for his scientific discoveries and theories regarding electricity. He invented the lightning rod, bifocal glasses, the Franklin stove, a carriage odometer and the first mechanical glass harmonica. He formed both the first public lending library in America *and* the first fire department in Pennsylvania.

Interestingly, much of Franklin's life was directed by a set of "virtues", based on his Puritan upbringing, which he noted in his diary. In addition to identifying particular virtues (what we would call "values" today), Franklin actively *defined* what they meant to him, so that he had a clear sense of how to live them on a daily basis.

Franklin was able to use his list of virtues as a kind of "moral compass" which guided him in his many endeavours and achievements.

Here are some of his virtues and the clarifying statement he created for each one. Although this example might seem quite archaic to us today, the aim of this exercise is for you to produce something similar for yourself.

Temperance: "Eat not to dullness; drink not to elevation."

Silence: "Speak not but what may benefit others or yourself; avoid trifling conversation."

Order: "Let all your things have their places; let each part of your business have its time."

Resolution: "Resolve to perform what you ought; perform without fail what you resolve."

Frugality: "Make no expense but to do good to others or yourself; i.e. waste nothing."

Industry: "Lose no time; be always employed in something useful; cut off all unnecessary actions."

Sincerity: "Use no hurtful deceit; think innocently and justly, and, if you speak, speak accordingly."

Justice: "Wrong none by doing injuries, or omitting the benefits that are your duty."

Moderation: "Avoid extremes; forbear resenting injuries so much as you think they deserve."

Cleanliness: "Tolerate no uncleanliness in body, clothes, or habitation."

Tranquillity: "Be not disturbed at trifles, or at accidents common or unavoidable."

Chastity: "Rarely use venery but for health or offspring, never to dullness, weakness, or the injury of your own or another's peace or reputation."

Record your list of values and their clarifying statements in your journal.

Now it's time to narrow things down a bit by looking specifically at how your values relate to your *working* life.

Clarifying Your Work Values

Work values are those that are intimately connected with the work you do and the career you build. Some may be universal in the sense that they matter in all areas of your life; others may apply only to your job. Don't be alarmed if your work values turn out to be significantly different from those in other areas of your life; this isn't unusual. For example, you may be quite easy-going and non-competitive at home, while at work you are highly competitive and always striving for victory.

This section is all about funnelling down to those values that are most important you *in the workplace*. We'll start uncovering your work values by using some self-coaching questions which help you to determine what matters most to you in the world. As ever, record your answers in your Vital Vocation Journal.

 Self-Coaching Questions

1. In terms of knowledge, what kind of information do you want to learn about or add to the world? What values might this knowledge serve?

2. In terms of humanity, where do you think the world needs more healing, compassion and justice? In which areas/countries/ social groups? What activities might help achieve this?

3. In terms of art and beauty, where would you like to see more of each? What kinds of art and beauty would you like to see more of? Why?

4. In terms of the planet, where do you feel more support, protection and development is needed? Which environmental challenges are particularly compelling or concerning to you? Why? Which values might help effect an improvement in this area?

 EXERCISE 9: Work Values

Taking into consideration what you've learned from the self-coaching questions above, go back through your original list of values and put an asterisk beside any of those that feel particularly relevant to you in a work/career context. If there are any values missing (check your answers to the self-coaching questions) add them to your list now.

Write clarifying statements for these work values, if you haven't already done so (see Exercise 8).

Clarifying Your Values by Job Type

Now, you have a list of values that are specifically aligned to your Vital Vocation. Let's refine them just a bit further, in a way that will help point you in the direction of the type of job/career that's perfect for you…

EXERCISE 10:
Grouping Your Values by Holland Code

This exercise will help you clarify your values and how they might be translated into a particular "type" of career. It's based on the Holland Code System, developed by the late psychologist John L. Holland.

Step 1

Consider the following six groups of value clusters. Look at each value statement in inverted commas and give it a score out of 10, depending on how important it is to you, with 1 being "not important to me" and 10 being "vitally important to me". Rank these individual scores, and make a note of your top five values statements overall in your journal.

Step 2

Now give each cluster a total score (by adding up the scores for each of the statements in that cluster) then use the scores to rank the clusters and list them, in their prioritised order, in your journal.

Value Clusters:

Cluster 1: It's important for me to...
"Be able to move around."
"Use my hands."
"Meet clear standards."
"See results."
"Work outdoors."

Cluster 2: It's important for me to...
"Be able to structure my own work."

"Be recognised for my knowledge."
"Contribute new learning to a field."
"Demonstrate a high degree of skill."
"Engage in complex questions and demanding tasks."

Cluster 3: It's important for me to…
"Be able to write or present ideas."
"Be free to express my uniqueness."
"Be involved in studying or creating beauty."
"Create new ideas, programmes or structures."
"Have personal control over my life and lifestyle."

Cluster 4: It's important for me to…
"Be involved in helping others directly."
"Contribute to the betterment of the world."
"Feel that my work is making a difference."
"Have opportunities for self-development."
"Work with others towards common goals."

Cluster 5: It's important for me to…
"Be able to get ahead rapidly."
"Be in a position to change opinions."
"Have a high standard of living."
"Have the power to influence others' activities."
"Impress others, have respect and status."

Cluster 6: It's important for me to…
"Carry out responsibilities and meet requirements."
"Complete work where attention to detail is required."
"Do work where employment is secure."
"Do work where tasks are clear."
"Have regular hours and predictable work."

Analysing Your Results

Firstly, simply notice which of the statements resonate most strongly with you. Are the statements in your top five all present in one cluster or spread across several? Which clusters stand out more than others? What do your top five statements tell you?

Then, consider the ranking of your clusters. In which order did you rank them? What do your scores tell you about the type of job that would appeal most to you? Use the key below to figure this out.

Key to the Clusters:

Cluster 1: You are likely to enjoy work that places value on athletic or mechanical ability and which allows you to work with objects, machines, tools, plants, animals, and/or be outdoors.

Cluster 2: You are likely to enjoy work that places value on the ability to observe, learn, investigate, analyse, evaluate or solve problems.

Cluster 3: You are likely to enjoy work that places value on artistic or innovative abilities, on the intuition, and which gives you the opportunity to work in situations that encourage you to use your imagination and creativity.

Cluster 4: You are likely to enjoy work that places value on the ability to work with people: to inform, teach, help, train, develop or communicate with them.

Cluster 5: You are likely to enjoy work which places value on the ability to perform in a way that generates wealth and which enables you to demonstrate your ability to influence, persuade, lead or manage people for economic or organisational gain.

Cluster 6: You are likely to enjoy work that places value on the ability to work with information, to demonstrate your administrative or numerical ability, to do detailed work and to follow through on other people's instructions.

We'll come back to the Holland Code System in the next chapter.

You've just unearthed some important and detailed information on your values! Let's start putting that information together.

 VITAL VOCATION ROUND-UP 2: Values

Step 1

Based on the information you've gathered in the preceding exercises, write yourself a Values Statement. It might look something like this:

*"The things that matter most to me in life are_____.
I think that these are important because_____. I think what the world needs most right now is_____. I believe the contribution I should be making is_____.
I am likely to enjoy work that places value on (insert details of appropriate Cluster description here)."*

Here's an example from one of my workshop participants, Mark:

"The things that matter most to me in life are adventure, excitement and innovation. I think that these are important because they stimulate new ideas and new ways of thinking. I think what the world needs most right now is new perspectives on tackling environmental and peacekeeping issues. I believe the contribution I should be making is to bring some original

ideas into the field of conflict resolution so that I can help support a fairer, more peaceful world. I am likely to enjoy work that places value on the ability to work with people: to inform, teach, help, train, develop or communicate with them."

Step 2

Take a clean page in your Vital Vocation Journal and give it the title, "Values". Write the list of your key values on this page, along with your own Values Statement and any other impressions you've received about your values.

Now you know what matters most to you. It's an important factor in finding your Vital Vocation - and you're another step closer to doing just that.

CHAPTER 4
ENVIRONMENT

Be careful the environment you choose for it will shape you; be careful the friends you choose for you will become like them.

~ W. Clement Stone

Finding the right working environment in which to use your talents and demonstrate your values is important – and achievable. The elements we'll be examining in detail in this chapter are:

People – the other human beings you want to work with and for

Place – the location in which you want to work

Workplace type – the kind of workplace that fits you best

Remuneration – the level of salary (and other rewards) you want and need in order to be comfortable, happy and secure

Let's take a look at each in turn.

Your Preferred People Environment

The quality of our relationships with work colleagues is a major factor in determining the quality of our work – and also the extent to which we're able to enjoy it. Good jobs can be blighted by unpleasant work colleagues, just as mundane jobs can be rendered bearable by the friendly people around us. Obviously, it's important to think specifically about the kind of people you want to be surrounded by. One of the most useful ways to do this is to find something called your Holland Code. Again, this is based on the work of the late psychologist John L. Holland, to whom we referred in Chapter 3.

Holland proposed that there were six principal "people environments", and each of us has three preferred environments among the six. They are:

1. **The "Realistic" People Environment**: This is populated mainly by people who prefer activities involving the ordered, systematic manipulation of objects, tools, machines and animals. These people like being in nature, taking part in athletics and/or using tools and machinery. This is the environment of **"doers"**.

2. **The "Investigative" People Environment**: This is populated mainly by people who prefer activities involving the observation and investigation of physical, biological and/or cultural phenomena. These people are curious and enjoy analysing things. This is the environment of **"thinkers"**.

3. **The "Artistic" People Environment**: This is populated mainly by people who prefer activities involving ambiguous, free, un-systematised activities which create art forms or products. These people are imaginative and innovative. This is the environment of **"creators"**.

4. **The "Social" People Environment**: This is populated mainly by people who prefer activities involving the manipulation and management of others to inform, train, develop, cure and/or enlighten them. These people are focused on helping and/or serving people. This is the environment of **"helpers"**.

5. **The "Enterprising" People Environment**: This is populated mainly by people who prefer activities involving the manipulation and management of others to attain organisational or personal goals. These people like to start projects and/or organisations, and like to influence people. This is the environment of **"persuaders"**.

6. **The "Conventional" People Environment**: This is populated mainly by people who prefer activities involving the ordered and systematic manipulation of data, such as keeping records, filing and reproducing materials, storing information and organising written, numerical and electronic data. These people enjoy detailed work and like to see tasks and projects through to completion. This is the environment of "**organisers**".

You may know immediately which of the above environments you fit best. The next exercise will help you if you don't know, or need to confirm your suspicions.

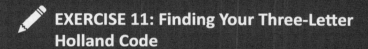

EXERCISE 11: Finding Your Three-Letter Holland Code

Step 1

Circle the number of any item below that appeals to you.

1. Working on a farm, growing things

2. Carrying out advanced mathematics

3. Acting in a play

4. Studying people in other countries

5. Talking to people at a social gathering

6. Using a word processor

7. Fixing a motor vehicle

8. Astronomy

9. Drawing or painting

10. Going to church

11. Working on a sales campaign

12. Using a cash register

13. Carpentry

14. Physics

15. Learning and using a foreign language

16. Teaching children

17. Buying clothes for a store

18. Working from nine to five

19. Setting type for a printer

20. Working in a chemistry laboratory

21. Reading art and music magazines

22. Helping people solve their personal problems

23. Selling life insurance

24. Typing reports

25. Driving a forklift truck

26. Using a chemistry set

27. Being around musicians

28. Making new friends

29. Training leaders

30. Planning and following a budget

31. Fixing electrical appliances

32. Building a model of a rocket

33. Creative writing

34. Attending sports events

35. Being elected class president

36. Using business machines

37. Building things

38. Doing puzzles in a magazine

39. Fashion design

40. Belonging to a club

41. Giving speeches or presentations

42. Keeping detailed records

Step 2

On the grid below, circle the numbers of the items that appealed to you most from the list above. Count the numbers circled in each row, reading across from left to right. How many have you circled in each row?

R=REALISTIC	1	7	13	19	25	31	37
I=INVESTIGATIVE	2	8	14	20	26	32	38
A=ARTISTIC	3	9	15	21	27	33	39
S=SOCIAL	4	10	16	22	28	34	40
E=ENTERPRISING	5	11	17	23	29	35	41
C=CONVENTIONAL	6	12	18	24	30	36	42

In which category did you score highest? Which did you score second highest? Third highest?

Write the letters of the three highest categories, in order. This is your Holland Code. For example, if you scored highest in "Social", second highest in "Artistic", and third highest in "Enterprising", your Holland Code is SAE.

Don't worry if you can't determine your third highest; just write the first and second highest. In this case, your Holland Code will be two letters, such as SA.

Step 3

In your journal, write out a statement about your ideal people environment, based on the code and the descriptors of each of the types, above.

For example, if your Holland Code was IAS, you'd write:

"I would like to work in an environment where I am surrounded by people who are very curious and like to investigate or analyse things (I). They should also be very innovative (A) and focused on trying to help or serve people (S)."

Step 4

Using your two- or three-letter Holland Code, consider the list of possible environments below. Remember, these are the environments where people with similar Holland Code preferences are likely to gather. What does your code tell you about which type of people environment you might enjoy working in? Bear in mind that these are just examples and it is by no means an exhaustive list. Record any useful impressions in your journal.

R = REALISTIC
Manufacturing; Trades; Catering; Computing; Printing

I=INVESTIGATIVE
Biotechnology; Chemistry; Engineering; Healthcare

A=ARTISTIC
Advertising; Journalism; Webmastery; Media; Graphics

S=SOCIAL
Management; Education; Hotels; Real Estate; Retail; Sales

E=ENTERPRISING
Business; Finance; Law; Accounting; Self-employment

C=CONVENTIONAL
Banking; Government; Insurance; Human Resources

Note: This exercise is based on the work of John Holland, as outlined in his book *Making Vocational Choices* (Psychological Assessment Resources Inc., 1997). It's a very worthwhile read if you're looking for a deeper exploration of the Holland Codes System.

Your Preferred Geographical Location

A useful question to answer in terms of geography is:

"Where would you most like to live and work – if you had a choice – besides where you are now?"

You may love or hate where you are now. Either way, you may in the future find yourself faced with an opportunity to consciously *choose* whether to stay or to go – and it pays to be prepared for that moment.

In answering the question above, you don't immediately need to come up with the name of a specific place. You just need to list the *geographical factors* that are important to you. Becoming clear about these can help you become clear about the possible locations in which they may be found. And when you find somewhere that fits the bill, because you're clear about the criteria you're looking for, you'll recognise it.

EXERCISE 12:
Finding Your Favourite Places

You'll need several pages in your journal for this exercise.

Step 1

List the names of all the places you have ever lived and worked. Write the name of each place at the top of a sheet of paper – one place per sheet of paper.

Step 2

Divide each sheet into two by drawing a line in the middle of the page, from top to bottom, making two columns. Head the first column "Negative Aspects" and the second one "Positive Aspects".

Step 3

In column one, make a list of all the factors you disliked and *still* dislike about that specific place. Keep writing until you've made a note of *all* the negative factors you can think of. Bullet points are fine, for example:

- "too cold"

- "unfriendly people"

- "too long a commute to work"

- "too far away from my family".

Step 4

In column two, turn each of the negative statements into a positive statement. For example, if you'd written *"too long a commute to work"*, you'd now write *"short and easy commute to work"*.

Step 5

When you've finished translating each negative into a positive, think of a few brand new positive statements that you'd like to be able to say about your ideal geographical environment. For example, if you hadn't mentioned anything about the weather in your negative statements, but feel that weather would be important in your ideal location, you might write *"has a pleasant climate"*.

Step 6

Rank your positive statements. Identify your top ten positive statements from the list and write them on a separate page in your journal headed "My Ideal Place of Work".

Step 7

Make a note of any places in the world which *you* can immediately think of that match as many of your top ten positive statements as possible. Write them on the page of your journal headed "My Ideal Place of Work".

Step 8

Find out which places in the world meet the criteria you've identified. Do some research on the internet. Show your list of ten prioritised, positive factors to everyone you know (and trust) and ask them what cities, towns, countries or places of work they know of that have all or most of these factors.

Step 9

From the names you generated in steps 7 and 8, choose the three that look most intriguing to you, and start finding out more about them. Google them. Read their Wikipedia entries. Buy a second-hand book about them from Amazon. Read articles about them in magazines. Subscribe to online job bulletins from these areas. Take action and begin to open your mind to these places, *always remembering that you're not obliged to move anywhere until you're ready.*

Step 10 (optional)

If you have a significant other to take into consideration – a child, a partner, an ageing parent – you can ask them to complete the exercise too, and combine your ranked lists, then look for locations that meet your combined criteria.

Step 11

Write a statement in your journal – "The parts of the world I would most like to live and work" – and list them.

Note: Remember it's fine if you don't want to move from where you are now. Maybe where you currently are is your preferred geographical environment. If that's so, that's fine. Just bear in mind that exactly how "ideal" it remains will be partly determined by the things you're discovering about the other factors of your Vital Vocation. You may discover that the place you live now fits beautifully with the other factors – or instead that these other factors point you to another place entirely (for example, if that's where jobs in your chosen field are most easily found). This exercise will help you think carefully about what other aspects of that potential environment you need to check out in order to ensure that it's right for you.

Getting Paid What You're Worth: Your Ideal Remuneration Level

Determining the right level of pay for the work you do can be a very personal matter. One person's reward is another's insult. A great deal depends on your means, the market and the general field in which you choose to work. The self-coaching questions that follow will help you to think about what your initial remuneration considerations should be.

 ## Self-Coaching Questions

1. At what level will you be working? CEO, director, manager, team leader, team member, partner, solo worker, self-employed?

3. What salary level should you be aiming at? You might like to consider this in terms of minimum and maximum. Minimum would be what you need just to "get by". Maximum could be any huge figure you can think of, but it is probably more useful to consider the salary you *realistically* could make (with your present level of competence and experience) were you working for a real, but generous, boss or company.

3. What salary range do your current budgetary pressures suggest to you? Make a budget template, including the following cost headings: housing, food, clothing, transport costs, insurance, medical expenses, support for family members, charitable donations, school/learning costs, pet care, monthly payments of bills and debts, taxes, savings, pensions, leisure/discretionary spending. From this, determine the total amount you need each month to cover these costs. Create two budgets: one containing the expenses you'd ideally like to be able to cover and the other, based on figures below which you cannot afford to go. The two figures give you your monthly salary range. (There's more detail about how to prepare a budget in Chapter 9.)

4. Consider what other rewards - besides money - your ideal job might offer you. These might be: adventure, challenge, respect, influence, popularity, fame, power, intellectual stimulation, opportunities to demonstrate leadership, creativity,

decisiveness, expertise or helpfulness. What other rewards can you think of? To what extent do these other potential rewards offset what you might require in terms of salary?

Preferred Working Conditions: Finding the Type of Work Environment in which You'll Thrive

There are several things to consider here. The following exercise and self-coaching questions will help you identify the working conditions that are most important to you.

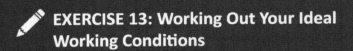

EXERCISE 13: Working Out Your Ideal Working Conditions

The best way to approach this is by starting with the things you *disliked* most about your previous jobs and – as you did when considering your preferred geographical locations – flipping these negative statements into positive ones. This will help you determine the type of conditions that are required in order for you to thrive.

Step 1

Divide a sheet of paper into four columns. Head them as follows:

- Places I have worked.

- Conditions I disliked in these places of work.

- Positive conditions: the keys to my effectiveness at work

- Prioritized working conditions

Step 2

In the first column, list all your jobs/places of work

Step 3

In the second column, next to each one, make a short list of the key conditions you disliked most in them: the conditions that inhibited your ability to do the job well.

Step 4

In the third column, write the opposites of the dislikes. You now have a list of the conditions you require if your effectiveness at work is to be at its maximum level.

Step 5

In the fourth column, rank these positive conditions. You can either use an online prioritiser, or your own instinct. Which of these conditions matter most to you?

To further clarify the kind of working environment you'll be happiest in, work through these self-coaching questions, jotting down notes and impressions in your journal.

 Self-Coaching Questions

1. **Pace**. Do you enjoy an environment that's busy and bustling, or steady and peaceful? How many hours do you want to work each week? How many days per week or month? How much time do you need to keep free in order to pursue your leisure activities and personal life (to a level that satisfies you)?

2. **Support**. You may like to experience a high level of independence in your work (the less direction, the better), or you may feel that your workplace needs to give you clear guidance and support in order for you to thrive. Consider the extent to which you'll need to feel a sense of significance at work, the need you have for autonomy or direction, and

the level of challenge you want to experience. Will company training and mentoring programmes be important to you?

3. **Company size**. If you're considering working for an organisation, do you work best alone or with co-workers? Do you prefer to feel part of a large organisation or a smaller one? Are you a team player or do you prefer to work alone? Do you want your work to be focused in one location, or should it range across several?

4. **Organisational culture**. Do you prefer a work environment that is conservative or radical, socially conscious or less so, employee-oriented or results-driven (and of course, the two aren't necessarily mutually exclusive). Do your prefer that the company has a clear vision or that it goes with the flow? To what extent do you expect/wish to have a direct influence on the culture?

Let's round up…

VITAL VOCATION ROUND-UP 3: Environment

Step 1

Based on the information you've gathered in the preceding exercises, write yourself an "Environment Statement". It might look something like:

"I will thrive in an environment where the people are_____, the location is_____, the working conditions are _____, and the salary and reward level is_____."

Here's an example from Helen, who participated in the *Vital Vocation Online Coaching Programme*:

"I will thrive in a fast-paced environment where the people are helpful, friendly, and cooperative the location is near my elderly parents' home, the working conditions are flexible (especially in terms of childcare) and the salary and reward level is well above average (although flexibility is more important to me than salary at this time)."

Step 2

List any other environmental considerations you've identified, including details of any specific *places* you identified in Exercise 12.

Now you know *where* your Vital Vocation might lie and you know the type of environment in which it might best be situated. Next, we'll look in a bit more detail at what you might be *doing* in this vocation. At last – it's time to look at your skills.

CHAPTER 5
SKILLS

The true test of lifelong learning is the extent to which we are able to go on knowing how to acquire skills during all life situations.

~ Anon

Sorting Your Skills

Exploring the big, important areas of talents, values and environment can be exhilarating – and exhausting – but I hope it's become apparent to you why I dropped you in at the deep end. The bottom line is this: you can't find the work you love by doing things you *don't* love. Finding the things that are most important to you is the first and most fundamental step on the path to your Vital Vocation – the one from which everything else flows.

Of course, once you're *in* your ideal job (or jobs), you're still going to have to be able to turn your hand to a range of things to get your work done on a day-to-day basis. So now it's time to get just a *bit* more practical. In this chapter, we're going to be unearthing the skills you can make use of on a day-to-day basis in whatever job or career you find yourself.

> *Our focus here will be to find the skills you most enjoy using. Finding work that requires you to use your most enjoyable skills on a regular basis is another great way building the combination of activities that constitutes your Vital Vocation.*

As I explained in Chapter 1, skills are those abilities you've developed over time and learned to carry out competently. They can either be *functional* (things you can *do* well) or *intellectual* (things you *know* a lot about).

In any job, you'll be expected to use a range of skills. Some of these you'll enjoy and some less so. You may even find that some skills are things you're perfectly competent at doing, but just don't *enjoy*. I'm competent at doing maths to prepare a complex budget, but frankly I'd sooner chew glass.

Obviously a "good" job for you will be one in which the balance is tipped towards the use of skills you enjoy (and finding those skills will be what we're going to focus on in this chapter), but here's something to bear in mind: if you're doing work based on your *talents* and *values*, in an *environment* you care about, then you'll probably find that you don't mind using your less-exciting skills.

You're in trouble when you're in a job that *isn't* based on things you care about *and* you have to use skills you don't enjoy. Such a situation is a recipe for restlessness and dissatisfaction. That won't be a problem for anyone who's on the path to their Vital Vocation, of course.

You may be thinking that it should be simple to find your skills and that you could quite easily write them all down in a list (you will have the opportunity to do just that in a moment), but I think you'll find that you have many more skills than you realise, so in this chapter I'm going to ask you to dig a bit deeper.

The important thing for our purposes is that we find out which of your current skills you enjoy using most, as well as which skills you might be most interested in developing within your chosen career.

Basic Skills Sorting

Let's start with that list!

EXERCISE 14: Your Simple Skills List

Below you'll find a Skills Checklist to help you assess which skills you possess. Go down the list of skills and make a note of any skills you think you *currently* possess. Don't just think about the skills you've previously used in work situations. The skills you use in your hobbies (e.g. organising), or to manage your home (e.g. managing finances), or in dealing with friends and loved ones (e.g. listening) all count.

This is simply about doing an initial trawl to discover the things you can do, or that you know about. Don't include anything you're not at least "quite good" at, even if it's a skill you think you *should* possess. In this exercise, you should tick *any* skills you possess - not just the ones you enjoy using.

If you know of any skills that you possess and which are missing from the list, make a note of them too.

Skills Checklist

Make a note of skills out of the following list:

Leadership:

Initiating projects, ideas and relationships

Self-governing

Managing change

Solving problems

Dealing with conflict

Taking risks

Making difficult decisions

Gaining the cooperation of others

Leading organised groups

Directing others

Winning the confidence of others

Intervening in crisis situations

Management:

Setting and achieving goals

Establishing priorities

Formulating and interpreting policy

Designing projects

Contributing to team-building

Delegating tasks

Managing time for self and others

Supervising others

Managing people and things

Anticipating future need

Coping with ambiguity

Communication:

Reading with comprehension

Editing effectively

Thinking quickly

Explaining concepts

Foreign language skills

Reporting accurately

Writing explicitly and concisely

Writing persuasively

Questioning effectively

Listening intently and accurately

Speaking convincingly

Using computers effectively

Using the internet and social media effectively

Attention to Detail:

Executing plans, instructions, decisions

Working within specified limits (e.g. budgets)

Handling several tasks simultaneously

Working under pressure

Identifying suitable resources

Acquiring resources effectively

Keeping information confidential

Attending to details

Showing perseverance

Tolerating monotony

Classifying, recording, filing, retrieving

Operating equipment (machinery, computers, etc.)

Influencing/Persuading:

Developing rapport/trust

Influencing attitudes/behaviours of others

Motivating others

Recruiting others with appropriate skills

Mediation

Negotiating/bargaining

Performing/Presenting/Art:

Getting up in front of a group

Showing confidence in public appearances

Speaking effectively in front of others

Stimulating enthusiasm in an audience

Using humour effectively

Playing sports

Directing public events

Acting

Singing

Dancing

Playing music

Illustrating/painting

Photography

Interior decorating

Choreographing dance and performance

Composing music

Manipulating materials

Dealing creatively with symbols

Creative writing

Using non-verbal communication well

Intuition/Innovation/Creation:

Demonstrating original imagination

Inventing processes/approaches

Inventing materials and resources

Creating programmes of information

Creating physical products

Perceiving intuitively

Understanding the arts

Serving/Helping/Healing:

Dealing effectively with the public

Being of service to others

Displaying sensitivity and caring

Relating to a variety of people

Healing others

Improving institutional environments

Working as a member of a team

Displaying patience/tact

Raising the self-esteem of others

Representing others accurately (liaising)

Protecting people/property

Researching/Investigating/Evaluating:

Informational interviewing

Designing and conducting surveys

Researching/investigating/analysing data

Diagnosing

Grasping and absorbing new information

Observing

Evaluating people

Evaluating procedures

Evaluating results

Reaching conclusions based on evidence

Instructing/Interpreting/Guiding:

Communicating information

Teaching

Coaching

Accepting and understanding differing opinions

Facilitating growth/development of others

Counselling and guiding decisions

Facilitating groups

Training others

Numerical/Financial Management:

Demonstrating a memory for numbers

Calculating/computing

Managing money

Keeping effectively financial records

Fiscal analysis/planning

Developing a budget

Managing a budget

Manipulating numbers effectively

Other Skills (add any you feel are missing):

You can use this list in the future - with your additions - to find the skills you need to develop. When you're in the position of embarking upon a new job or business, you'll have an idea of what's required of you. Take a look at the list and use it to make a note of any skills you don't currently possess, but feel you need. Those are the skills you'll either have to develop (through training, development and practice) or that you should outsource to other people (more on that tactic later).

The Scenarios (and Skills) of Your Life

Time to delve a bit deeper. Now we're going to start unearthing those skills that give you the most satisfaction. Remember, your Vital Vocation is founded on the skills you *enjoy* using, not just any skills which you *can* use. Because of that, it's important to prioritise.

EXERCISE 15: Skills Scenarios

Step 1: Select your scenarios

To complete this exercise, you will need to think about at least five scenarios from your past in which you carried out an activity just because it was fun or because it gave you a sense of adventure or enjoyment or accomplishment. It might help you to make some notes on each scenario. Take a fresh page in your journal for each.

For each scenario, you can pick something you did in or outside of work. In fact, try to balance the scenarios so that you have at least a couple from work and a couple from outside of work. You can think about anything from any period of your life, but try to pick several different periods over the five scenarios. It doesn't matter if anyone else knew of your sense of accomplishment or enjoyment or not.

The scenarios have to be those in which the skills you used helped you to achieve some sort of outcome (these are the kind of skills you need to use "on the job", after all); so you should think about why you were doing what you were doing, any **obstacles** you faced, the **detailed steps you took (including the skills you used)** to overcome those obstacles, and the result of your endeavours.

Try to choose scenarios in which you used a mixture of **functional** and **intellectual** skills. Or ensure that you choose a wide enough range of different scenarios so that each type of skill features in at least one of the scenarios. When you're detailing your skills, you can use the skills list above to give you ideas, or simply use your own skill descriptions.

When I used this exercise in a workshop, Matt chose this scenario from his schooldays:

The "why": I wanted to win the school talent competition with my friends, especially the cash prize. I got a couple of friends interested and we formed a musical group, and I was nominated to be the manager. I had a chance to demonstrate my intellectual skill of knowing how to write music, and composed a song to perform. I'd also be able to use my functional skill of playing the guitar.

The obstacles: We didn't have any proper instruments to play or practise with and couldn't afford decent costumes.

What I did: I approached the head of the music department and asked if we could borrow some instruments (a guitar, some drums and a keyboard). He was a bit reluctant to loan these out, so I assured him they'd be well looked after and brought a permission slip from my parents to show that they were aware of what I was asking to borrow. I also suggested that one of my friends ask his mother if she would make us some outfits to wear, if we pooled our pocket money and paid for materials. We were able to get the instruments and start practising, and by the date of the competition we were pretty good. We also had some nice colourful shirts that my friend's mother had made for us. We called ourselves The ColourTones and performed in the competition. We came third, which we were really pleased about because the people who won were really good.

The result: We didn't win the prize money, but we each got a little trophy.

Step 2: Extract your skills

Now go through your notes for each scenario and circle those words and phrases that demonstrate the skills you **most enjoyed** using in those scenarios. Remember, you've picked scenarios that were fun. Now, you're picking out the skills from those scenarios that you most enjoyed using – so you're really honing in on the skills that are most enjoyable for you. Don't circle anything that you didn't enjoy doing.

The "why": I wanted to win the school talent competition with my friends, especially the cash prize. I got a couple of friends interested and (we formed a musical group,)and I was nominated to be the manager. I had a chance to demonstrate my intellectual skill of knowing how to write music, and (composed a song to perform.) I'd also be able to use my functional skill of playing the guitar.

The obstacles: We didn't have any proper instruments to play or practise with and couldn't afford decent costumes.

What I did: I approached the head of the music department and asked if we could borrow some instruments (a guitar, some drums and a keyboard). He was a bit reluctant to loan these out, so I assured him they'd be well looked after and brought a permission slip from my parents to show that they were aware of what I was asking to borrow. I also suggested that one of my friends ask his mother if she would make us some outfits to wear, if we pooled our pocket money and paid for materials. We were able to get the instruments and start practising, and by the date of the competition we were pretty good. We also had some nice colourful shirts that my friend's mother had made for us. We called ourselves The ColourTones and performed in the competition. We came third, which we were really pleased about because the people who won were really good.

The result: We didn't win the prize money, but we each got a little trophy.

As an example, here are some of the words Matt circled in his scenario above, and the skills they represent:

- **Formed a musical group** *("Initiating projects, ideas and relationships")*
- **Composed a song to perform** *("Composing music")*
- **Approached the head of music and asked if we could borrow some instruments** *("Solving problems")*
- **Suggested that one of my friends ask his mother if she would make us some outfits to wear, if we pooled our pocket money and paid for materials** *("Gaining the cooperation of others"* and *"Inventing materials and resources")*
- **We called ourselves The ColourTones and performed in the competition.** *("Working as a member of a team").*

Step 4: Rank your skills

To gather a picture of the skills that are most important to you and that you most enjoy using, look at the different skills you used across all the scenarios (remember, you're only circling those you most enjoyed using) and notice which of them stand out for you again and again. If you only thought of five scenarios and are struggling to find a pattern of skills, try to recall a couple more, and go through the process of extracting the skills from these scenarios. Make a list of all the skills you used, and rank them in order – with most-used skills at the top.

VITAL VOCATION ROUND-UP 4: Skills

After you've ranked your skills, copy the list into a fresh page of your journal, under the heading "Skills".

Using your list of prioritized skills, write a Skills Statement:

"I will thrive in an environment which enables me to use my favourite skills, which are...(list them in order)."

Now you know which skills you possess – probably more than you realised – and can use should you need to. Crucially, you've also identified which skills you *most* enjoy using.

"But What If I *Don't* Enjoy Using These Skills?"

When approaching your Vital Vocation, a general rule of thumb is to focus on using those skills you most enjoy, and minimize having to use those you don't enjoy. Those skills should – if possible – be outsourced, or delegated.

Some jobs simply require the use of certain skills, and it may be that some of those skills just aren't going to be fun for you. In cases like this, you need to look at the bigger picture. If 90% requires the use of skills you enjoy, you may be able to put up with the 10% that doesn't turn you on.

However, I strongly recommend that – if you *possibly* can - you outsource any tasks which require you to use skills that you really don't enjoy using.

There are a couple of important reasons for this. Firstly, you'll free up time for yourself to use the skills you *do* enjoy, and that way you'll be playing to your strengths. Trying to force yourself to do things you're not naturally good at is a hugely inefficient way of working.

Secondly, it gives someone who *is* good at those things the chance to shine. As I mentioned earlier, I can prepare a complex budget if I need to, but it's not something I'd choose to do if left to my own devices; and if I have to do it, the results are likely to be little more than competent.

I'd rather hire people who *love* finances and who thoroughly enjoy preparing complex budgets. I hire the very best people I can afford with the resources available to me, and let them get on with doing an excellent job. It never ceases to amaze me that there are people in the world who get a kick out of preparing and analysing financial data. To me, they're almost like an alien race. But boy, do I love them!

 ## Self-Coaching Questions

This has been a fairly intensive chapter, with a significant amount of writing and analysis, so I'm keeping it short. We finish with some questions for you to ponder. Remember to write the answers in your Vital Vocation Journal.

1. What kind of things/tasks/favours do people consistently ask you to do for them?

2. Which of your skills do others consistently recognise as being valuable?

3. What can you do, or do in a unique way, that almost no one else you know can do?

4. Which of the skills you possess have been most useful to you so far in life - and why?

5. Based on what you already know about your possible Vital Vocation, which skills (that you don't currently possess) might you need to gain? How might you go about gaining them?

CHAPTER 6
PUTTING IT TOGETHER:
THE EMERGING OUTLINE OF YOUR
VITAL VOCATION

A vision's just a vision
If it's only in your head.
If no one gets to see it,
It's as good as dead.
It has to come to light...

~ Stephen Sondheim,
Sunday in the Park with George

This is a brief but important chapter. Don't be tempted to skip it. It might seem hard to believe but, if you've been working through the process as outlined in the preceding chapters, you've come a *very* long way since the book began and you're ready to build up the full picture of your Vital Vocation. You don't have to know *precisely* what that vocation is yet (although it's fine if you do) and you don't have to create a perfectly detailed picture in order to move forward.

The first thing to do is simply pull together all the information you've gathered whilst examining the four factors of your Vital Vocation. By piecing these together, you'll build up a picture that you can use to move yourself powerfully forward in finding the work of your dreams.

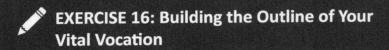

EXERCISE 16: Building the Outline of Your Vital Vocation

Review your previous notes and, in any way that feels right to you, start pulling together the information from each of the chapter "Round-Ups".

Option 1

The simplest way to do this is to transfer each of the statements you wrote in the "Vital Vocation Round-Up" sections onto a single clean page. Combined, these statements describe the outline of your Vital Vocation. You could use the Vital Vocation Worksheet format below:

VITAL VOCATION WORKSHEET

1: TALENTS Statement	2: VALUES Statement
3: ENVIRONMENT Statement	4: SKILLS Statement

Possible Vital Vocations (make a list).

What do the statements you've written immediately suggest to you about what your Vital Vocation could be? Jot your ideas down under your statement.

Option 2:

You may choose to approach this exercise in a slightly more "free-form" way. If it feels right to you, try writing keywords or listing the key things you discovered about each factor; or - if you're artistically inclined - you could take a large sheet of paper and make a *literal* picture, either by drawing, painting and/or sticking magazine cuttings onto the paper.

Whichever option you choose, the key thing is to make sure that what you end up with is a visual or written representation of the key components of your Vital Vocation. Remember, it can be a combination of one or more jobs and hobbies – as long as it enables you to make a living *and* pursue your passion. If you need to remind yourself, take a look at the section called *The Two Paths to a Vital Vocation* in Chapter 1.

At this point, take a moment to check in with yourself. Does the picture (whether it's in words or images) "feel" right? Do you recognise yourself – your gifts, dreams, ideas, abilities, aspirations – in it, even if you don't quite know what it's ultimately going to become?

If so, great. If not, it could be because you're still unsure of exactly where this is going to lead or because you're experiencing some resistance. Don't worry; we'll be looking at some very effective ways of dealing with internal and external obstacles in later chapters.

If, however, you *know* that the picture is way off beam, you may want to go back and review some of the exercises. Have you done them as thoroughly as you could? Have you been *really* honest with yourself in answering the self-coaching questions?

I invite and encourage you to complete this exercise, even if you've already figured out what your Vital Vocation is going to be.

If you *do* know what it is already, that's great and it's worth taking some time to celebrate the fact and really "cement" it in your consciousness. This is no small thing. If you *don't* know and if the picture you've just built still hasn't given you a blinding flash of inspiration, please don't worry. Take some time over the process and even if it doesn't make sense to you yet, give yourself time to assimilate the combination of all the work you've done so far. It's what all the previous chapters have been building up to and even if you don't quite know how that picture will be transformed into a real, practical vocation and way of life, trust me that the work you've done won't go to waste.

Making it Real

If you already know what your Vital Vocation is, you can skip the next exercise. If, however, you don't, here's where we start focusing down on some specifics. We'll use the outline you've created as a touchstone for identifying what your Vital Vocation might actually be. Think of it as the frame of a house – one that's waiting for plasterboard, bricks, mortar, a roof, windows, and a door...

 EXERCISE 17: Filling in the Gaps

Step 1:

First of all, take a look at your outline, whether it's in written or visual form. What does it suggest to you *immediately* in terms of possible jobs, careers or businesses (and remember it can be a combination of more than one of these)? Make a note in your journal of all your ideas. You may have to do this and then set the list aside for a while. When you come back to it, does anything in particular jump out at you? This isn't an exact science; the idea is to just give yourself some ideas.

See if you can list at least ten ideas of what you could do for a living in line with your Vital Vocation as it's described in your outline. Remember, that could include having a "good enough job" and pursuing your passion in the free time it affords you.

Step 2:

Explore the wonderful free site www.icould.com – it contains thousands of videos of people describing hundreds of different (and some quite unusual) careers. Use the information you've gathered about your Vital Vocation to suggest keywords you can use as search terms. Pop them into the search box, watch some videos, and start making notes of the careers that turn you on the most.

Step 3:

If you need some help, ask some trusted friends or colleagues for their ideas, based on your framework.

Again, you shouldn't worry if you are still unable to specify an exact vocation. That's not a failing on your part; it could be that your ideal work hasn't been invented yet because we're waiting for you to invent it!

"But What If I *Still* Don't Know?"

If your picture *is* still just an outline and you don't quite know what to head for, the answer to that is simple and, I promise you, very effective. You're going to pick *something* that feels exciting to you (based as far as possible on the picture you have built) and you're going to start heading towards it. In other words, even if your picture isn't very detailed, you're going to pick a target that feels as close as possible to your Vital Vocation and you're going to use that as a goal.

Let's say the themes of "communicating", "teaching", "speaking to audiences" and "conveying information" have come up for you again and again. Those themes may suggest becoming a teacher. Or they may suggest becoming a motivational speaker. Or an author who does occasional public speaking engagements. Or a tour guide. Or a university lecturer. If none of those occupations leaps out at you, does that matter? No. Just choose one – whichever one feels most interesting at this particular moment – and start moving towards it. Learn about it. Speak to others who are already doing it. Explore the career opportunities that exist around it.

Why? Well, by now you'll know that I believe that taking action – in *any* direction – is one of the very best ways of discovering what life has to offer you. Use the information you've gathered to set your direction, get moving and you're probably going to find that your Vital Vocation comes looking for you. Remember what I said right at the beginning of the book:

> *Sometimes, you just have to strike out in the vague direction of your dream, even if you don't know exactly where the journey's going to lead you. The very act of making the trip can reveal all the pieces that are missing.*

A Big Self-Coaching Question

Here's another prompt for you. So far, we've used groups of self-coaching questions to coax information and inspiration out from inside you. This time, I'm going to ask you just one question – because it's a big one.

I suggest you take some time – maybe even a few *days* – to ponder this question. This is big-picture, meaning-of-life stuff. Consider it in the context of everything you've learned so far. Read through your Vital Vocation Journal as you think about it. Look at the insights you've gained as you've worked through the book so far, and give yourself time to deeply reflect.

Just ask the question, give yourself some time, and see what answers arise. Here's the question:

> *If every experience of your life had been planned to train you for a specific "destiny" - what would you say your life thus far has prepared you to do?*

Taking The Next Step

Now that you have a picture of you Vital Vocation – no matter how clear or murky that picture is – we're going to start moving you towards *getting it.*

The second part of the book deals with this in detail and will help you pull together a practical, tactical plan that's going to move you into fast-forward mode in terms of finding your ideal work. Before then, we'll take some time to look at how to deal with any feelings of doubt or insecurity you may be feeling (Chapter 8).

But before all of that, you're going to do something that all the show business greats do to maximize their chances of a hit – you're going to stage a dress rehearsal.

CHAPTER 7
A DRESS REHEARSAL FOR YOUR DREAM JOB

*The world's a stage and most of us are
desperately unrehearsed.*

~ *Sean O'Casey*

Practice, Practice

Perhaps you've been wondering how some of the theoretical work done so far is going to be turned into practical action. Well, the time has come. You're going to start getting down to practicalities by doing something that's a lot of fun, and highly instructive. You're going to throw yourself a dress rehearsal.

No major play or musical performance gets underway without the company putting on a practice performance first. It's an essential part of building a perfect finished product. By uncovering any unforeseen glitches, the dress rehearsal allows the director to correct things so the opening night goes without a hitch.

Since finding your Vital Vocation is all about ensuring that *you're* the director of your own career destiny, that's what you're going to be doing in this chapter – throwing a dress rehearsal for your dream job or career.

Getting started is simple. You just need to pick a job or business (or a combination of several) as a practice goal; it doesn't have to be the "dream job" you've been uncovering as you've worked your way through this book, but it *must* be something that you have at least some degree of enthusiasm for. You then need to start taking purposeful steps towards getting it, just as if you were going after it for real.

It's a short chapter because you're going to have some very specific homework to do and I want you to get started as soon as you can.

The Nine Reasons You Should Have a Dress Rehearsal

The point here is to go through a trial run of choosing a job and then pulling together a plan to get it. Doing this will achieve several things for you:

1. It'll help you discover what obstacles might trip you up when you go after the "real thing" so you can deal with them when the time comes (you'll be learning how to deal with obstacles in chapters 8, 10 and 11).

2. It'll move you into practical-action mode, powerfully propelling you forward from the theoretical work of the last few chapters.

3. It'll bring you into contact with real people and this in turn will almost certainly help you generate more ideas and leads.

4. It'll give you the opportunity to discover and appreciate just how much help is actually out there when you decide to look for it (believe me, you're going to be pleasantly surprised).

5. It'll enable you to discover what job-search or business-building strategies might work best for you (and which won't).

6. It'll flush out the form that your own inner obstacles take so that you'll be able to apply the techniques you've already learned to deal with these most effectively.

7. It'll enable you to find out more about the support systems you're going to need so that you can start building them for yourself *before* you go after your real goal.

8. It'll give you a chance to consider what you definitely *don't* want to include as part of your Vital Vocation.

9. It'll enable you to try out some of the planning techniques

you'll be using in Part 2.

I told you it would be useful! Let's get started...

 EXERCISE 18: Planning Your Practice

Step 1: Pick a Goal, Any Goal

Your task here is to pick a job goal based on two elements: job *type* and job *location*. This doesn't have to be the job you really want (although it can be if you know what your Vital Vocation is already). And it doesn't have to be in the location you ultimately desire; but again, it can be if you know where that is. The important thing is that your practice goal is able to stir up a significant amount of enthusiasm within you. Bear in mind that your Vital Vocation can be a combination of a "good-enough job" and a range of hobbies and interests that make you happy, so your practice goal can be a similar combination.

You're then going to act as if this *is* your ideal job in your ideal location and you're going to *begin the process of getting it*.

"Help! I Can't Think of Anything!"

If you're struggling to decide what to choose, try one (or all) of these techniques to help you along:

- **Ask people**. Give them the outline of your Vital Vocation so far and ask them for suggestions as to jobs that might fit. You could do this with individual trusted friends or in a group setting.

- **Search the internet**. Take your lists of talents, skills and values as keywords, along with the words "job" and "career" and the name of your chosen practice location;

type them into Google and see what comes up.

- **Read**. If you have a rough idea of the field you're going to choose, go to the library and browse books and trade journals for that career area.

- **Fantasise**. Since this is a practice goal, you can afford to be a bit adventurous. As long as the goal you pick is a job that you can feel enthusiastic about and can realistically imagine doing, it can be anything – even something you don't feel you'd stick at forever. Don't be afraid to push the boat out with this one; who knows what you might discover?

Once you've chosen both your job type and job location (for example "Pet shop manager in Albuquerque") you're ready to move on to staging that dress rehearsal.

Step 2: Field Trip

Now comes the fun part. Having chosen your practice job type and job location, it's time to take a fun field trip into your ideal work - one that you can take without having to make any long-term commitments.

For the next week (or however long you'd like to give yourself between this chapter and the next one) you're going to *research your practice job* and then you're going to *take some specific steps towards getting it.*

In essence, you're going to stop just short of actually getting a job as a result of this exercise. However, I should tell you at this point that some of my clients actually *have* landed real work as a result of carrying out this exercise. Some of them have even stuck at these jobs long-term. Just remember that that's not the point of this exercise; the point is to give you some practice.

Here's how to do it, step-by-step:

1. **Gather information.** Find out as much as you can about the local community based in the area you've chosen and about the job market in that area. Again, the internet will be your friend in this regard. Research, research, research – and write everything you learn in your journal.

   Most importantly, make a list of all the possible places and people who may be of interest to you in your practice job search. Then, jot down some ideas about how you might investigate these areas when you make your field trip. Where will you start? Who might be able to give you the best clues about where else and who else might give you the information you need?

2. **Carry out a "virtual visit".** Call or write/email the key people who may be able to help you. If your ideal job is likely to be based in a particular company, try to arrange to speak to someone in that company (preferably the person with the power to hire and fire) and interview them about job prospects. This could be done on the phone or in person in step 3.

   If no vacancies are currently available, ask for a general discussion anyway. If you're worried about not getting through, be prepared to tell a little white lie – perhaps that you're researching their company for an article or further education project you're working on. Be polite and respectful, but don't pass up this opportunity to practise speaking to someone about a particular career area. This is a skill that will stand you in great stead in the future.

   By the way, another good place to contact is the local chamber of commerce (from a job market point of view) and the local tourist office (for information on the area). They may even be able to send you useful background information.

3. **Carry out a real visit**. This is why (for the purpose of

this exercise) it's useful to pick a location that's currently near you. Now that you have some information, take yourself to the area you've chosen and (if possible) into contact with people connected to the job type you've chosen. Pretend that this place is your ideal place. With as much curiosity as you can gather, uncover as much information as you can to help you land a job there. Examine everything with the eyes and ears of someone who is totally open; what do you notice about this place? What can you learn about the practice career you've chosen?

Speak to people; both those you've pre-arranged to speak to and others that you randomly meet. Ask them questions about the place and about themselves. Let them know about your interests and invite them to suggest who else you should speak to and where else you might go. Don't be afraid to try this; you might be surprised at what you can find out. If you have a business card, don't be afraid to give it to them. If you haven't, consider getting one made in time for the visit.

4. **Record what you learn**. Write down as much as you can about what you're learning during your dress rehearsal. Save leaflets and newspapers from your visit. Cut out interesting articles from the local press (that are relevant to your practice run) and stick them in your journal.

   Make sure you note the names of the people you spoke to and make a record of their contact details if you have them. Consider sending them a very brief thank-you note for their time and assistance (I strongly recommend that you do this. Some of these people may turn out to be important contacts for the future).

5. **Plan your application**. Take a look ahead at Part 2 of this book. Read through the information in Chapters 10 and 11 on dealing with external obstacles . Apply

this information to your practice goal. These are the techniques you'll be using for your *real* goal, so it's a good idea to get used to them at this point.

6. **"Apply"**. This is an optional extra. If you have the time and inclination, and if there is an interesting job going in your practice field and location – consider applying for it (use the information in Chapter 12 to help you). Or, at least, consider going through the process, even if you decide not to submit the application.

Why should you do this? Simply because it will be useful practice based on real information – the information you gathered during your field trip. Even if you don't go all the way, you'll almost certainly learn a lot from the process. And you never know what might happen.

When I coached Robert to work through this stage in the process, he *did* submit his application - "I decided I might as well, since I'd filled it in," he said - and got the job! It's a job he's still doing now and he loves it. Needless to say, Robert's practice area turned out to be close to the area of his Vital Vocation, which is not uncommon. However, it's not essential. You'll still gather great information, even if this process remains what it started out as – a trial run.

Once you've completed Exercise 18, use the following self-coaching questions to help you analyse the experience. As ever, record the answers in your journal.

 ## Self-Coaching Questions

1. In general, what did you learn during your dress rehearsal?

2. What do you know now about the type of environment you'd like to work in?

3. What have you gained in any new contacts you've made? Which

of these, if any, might be useful to you in finding your real Vital Vocation?

4. How close to your real Vital Vocation did this dress rehearsal feel? What would need to change in order for it to be as close to your Vital Vocation as possible?

5. What surprised you during this dress rehearsal?

6. What did you find most daunting about the process? How can you make yourself feel more comfortable when you're going after the real thing?

7. What do you feel are the key potential obstacles standing between you and your Vital Vocation? What information/ support will you need to prepare in order to deal with them?

8. What personal strengths did you discover in this exercise?

Going Deeper

If you want to take this concept of staging a dress rehearsal to a whole other level, you may find the following options useful.

- **Take a "vocation vacation".** This company offers opportunities for individuals to test drive the job of their dreams. Focused mainly in America, with some worldwide links, they provide mentoring schemes covering around 125 careers. They are definitely worth checking out if you want to take a field trip that lasts longer than a week!

  Vocation Vacations: http://vocationvacations.com/

  Other options for giving a job or a career test-drive before you commit to it include interviewing and job-shadowing people who are already in that job, or applying for an internship placement (if one is offered for the career you're interested in).

- **Volunteer.** As chief executive of one of the UK's leading volunteering charities (www.bvsc.org) and someone who has benefited greatly from the experience of volunteering, I have no hesitation in recommending voluntary work as an excellent way of testing out possible careers. In fact, I'm convinced that volunteering landed me my first job in the charitable sector (as a fundraiser). I had management experience in retail – working for the renowned Marks & Spencer – but it was my weekends and evenings spent doing community volunteering with young disadvantaged people that impressed the panel enough to offer me the job that changed my life. Check out your local Volunteer Centre, or search for volunteering opportunities online:

Do-It: Volunteering Made Easy (UK): http://www.do-it.org.uk/

Volunteering In America (USA): http://www.volunteeringinamerica.gov/

Voluntary Service Overseas (Europe & other territories): http://www.vso.org.uk/

CHAPTER 8
OVERCOMING YOUR
INTERNAL OBSTACLES

We will either find a way or make one.

~ Hannibal

If you're like most of my coaching clients – and like me – you've probably discovered that the very act of taking the steps outlined in the preceding chapters causes something strange to happen.

Are you experiencing some powerful feelings of unease and a sense that moving forward will be hard, if not impossible, for you? Perhaps these feelings have manifested themselves as anxiety after completing the exercises, or a strong desire to procrastinate before beginning the exercises, or even in a complete inability to start the exercises in the first place.

Relax! All is as it should be. Would it shock you to learn that I'm *hoping* that you've had this experience? Dear reader, it's not that I'm a sadist, but one of the reasons I plunged you straight in at the deep end was because I hoped that doing so would bring your own particular brand of internal resistance out into clear view, where we can deal with it. That's also why I've insisted you carry out the dress rehearsal outlined in Chapter 7.

If at any point you've felt like flinging this book against the wall then I've done my job well. Now that your resistance is out in the open, let's get on with dealing with it.

"Internal obstacles" are any of those uncomfortable feelings that rise up inside us during times of effort and stress, stopping us dead in our tracks. They're not "real" obstacles in the sense of those that exist in the outside world – like a tough economy, an unsupportive partner or an angry boss – but they're no less powerful for that. Just because they originate from inside you doesn't mean they can be easily dismissed. In fact, these can be the most powerful and tenacious obstacles of all.

This chapter will help you deal with them, and once you've mastered the techniques herein, you'll be able to apply them to *any* goal you're trying to pursue, job-related or otherwise. You'll also be able to refer back to this chapter when you need a reminder of how to tackle any internal obstacle.

By the way, we will be looking at how to deal with *external* obstacles in later chapters, so all your bases are covered.

The Advantage of Internal Obstacles

The good news is that internal obstacles *always* appear for a reason, and when they do, your first task is to uncover those reasons so that you can use that information to your advantage. That's *always* possible, I promise you.

In fact, you're about to learn why internal obstacles are the job-hunter's best friend. Rather than fear them, you may even learn to welcome them, safe in the knowledge that they're giving you an indication of some unfinished business which you need to attend to before moving forward. As the cartoonist Frank Tyger once said, "Opportunity's favourite disguise is trouble."

We're going to take a look at the following four broad categories of internal obstacle and some "blockbuster strategies" for getting past each of them:

- The **demotivation** that sabotages your enthusiasm
- The **procrastination** that stops you from getting started
- The **false assumptions** that make you talk yourself out of your goal

- The feelings of **stress** that can derail you on your journey to your Vital Vocation

Yes, internal resistance comes in various shapes and sizes. Consequently, this is the longest chapter of the book. I suggest you make yourself a drink and settle into your favourite chair with your pen and Vital Vocation Journal close beside you, and read on. Or select the strategy most appropriate to your own particular form of internal obstacle.

Let's bust some blocks!

Blockbuster Strategy 1: Dealing With Demotivation

Building Your Own Brand of Motivation

If you're feeling demotivated, unable to muster the enthusiasm to even start trying to find your dream job (maybe to the extent that you're not even motivated to start figuring out *how* to start trying), then you're probably wondering how on earth to change things. What's the secret to finding motivation? At the risk of disappointing you: there isn't one.

There's no "right" way to motivate yourself to make progress or to get yourself back on track when you become derailed. The only important thing is to find the ways which work best for you. Don't let anyone – including me – lead you to believe that there's a "secret motivational formula" which, if only you could find it, would enable you to sail effortlessly into the future.

What is motivation, anyway? We all know when we have it, and when we don't. When it's missing, we chide ourselves in the hope that that will make it appear again. The dictionary defines it for us as "the internal condition that activates behaviour and gives it direction". In our society, we're often told – explicitly and implicitly – that without motivation, nothing would ever get done, and that if we don't have it, we won't amount to anything. No wonder this mysterious motivation stuff is so sought after!

Yet, despite the constant quest for the Holy Grail of motivation, it isn't something we can ever find because it isn't something that exists "out there". The truth is that *motivation is the state that naturally arises when our desire for something – or to do something – overrides our desire to stay put.* When that happens, we find ourselves moving forward effortlessly, almost mindlessly, in a natural flow of action, often accompanied by feelings of excitement, expectation and pleasure. That's motivation!

> *If there is a secret, it's this: motivation can't be found, but it can be generated.*

In fact, looking around for motivation when it isn't there is a sure-fire way of making ourselves feel woefully *un*motivated, because it leads us to focus on what we lack. This fruitless quest usually just makes us painfully aware of the fact that we're not in action yet. If we feel that we should be in action when we're not, feelings of discomfort – guilt, frustration, depression, anger – tend to be the result. And so the vicious circle continues unabated.

Can you make yourself want something, before you do? No. Neither can I. Everything in its time. When the desire/inertia equation tips in the favour of desire, you'll start moving, and not a minute before. So, how do you stack the motivation equation in your favour? First, make peace with your demotivation. Then, take steps to awaken your desire.

Here's how:

Making Peace with Demotivation

One of the most important things to do when you're feeling demotivated is to respect your inertia. When you're not motivated, don't jump to the immediate conclusion that you *should* be. Take time to tune into why you feel the way you do. There could be a valid reason. It could be that your energy levels are low and that you need a rest before you charge off in the direction of your dream. You wouldn't set out on a long, fast journey in your car with no oil, little fuel and a rusty engine, would you? No – you'd have the engine tuned and oiled, and the tank filled. Afford yourself the same respect and common sense, and take some rest and recuperation if you need it.

If you're actively demotivated – that is, if you feel yourself actually *resisting* moving towards something – again, ask yourself why. Do you really want the thing you're trying to get motivated about, or do you just *want* to want it? There's a difference and you won't be able to properly awaken your desire until you know which position you're in. Also consider this: no one else can be motivated on your behalf, but are you being pushed to want something that someone close to you thinks you "should" want? Are you unconsciously bowing to peer pressure?

Awakening Your Desire

To awaken desire, you need to focus in on what you stand to gain from moving forward. By all means, focus on the ultimate goal, but you must focus on the small steps too. In fact, it's best to find the *smallest unit of gain* you possibly can and focus on building your desire for *that*.

Here's a non-job-related example: if you start working out to lose weight and get fit, your ultimate goal – a fit, healthy body – may be some way away, depending on where you're starting from. If your desire for it is strong enough, you'll be prepared to work out in all weathers and forego your favourite sweet treats. But what if your desire is dimmed by the fact that that ultimate goal seems so very far away? You need to find a benefit even closer to home in space and time: for example, how good you feel every time you work out or eat a healthy meal.

The "smallest unit of gain" isn't the perfect body – it's the great feeling you have as soon as you get off the treadmill or roll up your yoga mat. By going after *that* you put yourself on the path to your ultimate goal – and so it is with finding your Vital Vocation.

So, the next time you have big task to tackle, such as a dissertation to write, don't sit staring blankly at a pile of paper; pick up just one sheet and look forward, with all your heart, to the feeling you'll have when you've written just one sentence. Love it for its own sake and write it. Then write the next for the same reason, and the next, and the next. Before long, you'll have the first of many pages and you'll be on your way.

EXERCISE 19: Creating Motivation

Step 1

For the purposes of this exercise, pick any large-ish goal that you haven't got round to achieving: something you want to do but don't feel 100% motivated about yet. It doesn't have to be career-related, but it can be. It could be to create art, to get fit, to be more sociable, to draw up your family tree - anything as long as you genuinely desire it and haven't managed to muster up the enthusiasm you need to get going with it.

Step 2

Once you've decided on your goal, sit quietly, take a deep breath, get very still and ask yourself: "What's the *smallest unit of gain* I'm genuinely prepared to go after?" In other words, what *little thing* would you be *genuinely willing* to do in order to move closer to achieving your chosen goal? It must be something you are really willing to do; if you have any doubts, you need to think of something even smaller.

So, for example, if your goal was to create art, you may decide that your smallest unit of gain would be to paint a single picture. But if you don't *genuinely* feel willing to commit to that, you have to find something you *can* commit to, like buying some paintbrushes and watercolours. Maybe even the thought of that leaves you feeling unenthusiastic, or perhaps makes you nervous. So, maybe you need to start by merely looking at paints in a catalogue. Could you do that? Keep whittling down until you find the single thing you're willing to do.

Step 3

Do it!

Step 4

Make a note in your journal of how you felt while doing it - and how you felt afterwards. Did you feel scared? Disinterested? Excited? Sad? Worried? Confused? Clearer? More enthusiastic?

Step 5

Make a note of what *next* thing you could do as a follow on from that to take you a bit further towards your goal, and repeat steps 2–4. Make a note of how you feel, and – most importantly – take time to consider how motivated, or otherwise, you feel. In most cases, you'll probably find that the flame of motivation has at least been kindled. It may be small and it may need some gentle fanning for some time, but it's there. If it *isn't* there, you may need to consider whether you're being blocked by one of the other internal obstacles. If not, you may need to question whether you're going after something that you really want.

Step 6

Once you've mastered this process with this first goal, try applying it to the process of finding your Vital Vocation. What's the *smallest unit of gain* you're prepared to go after in finding or creating your ideal work?

Way down deep, we're all motivated by the same urges. Cats have the courage to live by them.

~ Jim Davis

Motivation is in the doing.

~ Susan Powter

Blockbuster Strategy 2: Getting Past Procrastination

Nothing is so fatiguing as the eternal hanging on of an uncompleted task.

~ William James

Do you find yourself regularly putting off doing things, even the things you know you'd enjoy if you just got on and did them? This strange phenomenon – of delaying important tasks or projects, stopping no sooner than you've started or suddenly finding a hundred other things you could be doing instead – seems to be a universal one. We've all procrastinated at some point or another. Show me someone who says they haven't and I'll show you a fluent liar.

It's quite explicable in some cases – for example when we're faced with doing something genuinely boring, painful or hard – but not in others. Doesn't it seem odd that we'd put off doing the very things that can bring us happiness, such as going after a cherished dream, long-held ambition or our ideal career? Yet we do exactly that, repeatedly.

Procrastination Doesn't Arrive Alone

The negative effects of chronic procrastination are no small matter. There's the growing sense of underachievement: of never really getting off the starting blocks of life. There's the uneasy feeling of standing still, even falling behind, as life whizzes ahead of us. Worst of all, there's the gnawing torture of self-reproach as guilty feelings surface to tell us that, since we can't seem to get our act together and do the things that others have no problem doing, we must be incompetent, stupid or lazy.

But if procrastination is such a bad egg, why on earth do we do it?

<u>What Procrastination *Isn't*</u>

Before we consider what procrastination is (and some strategies for dealing with it), let's get something straight regarding what it isn't. Namely, it isn't laziness.

I don't believe in laziness. If you're not doing something – including finding your Vital Vocation - it's either because you don't want to or because you believe you can't. Inherent laziness would result in an inability to make an effort under *any* circumstance, but just watch how fast you move when you're heading towards something you really want (and which presents no real conflict for you).

Ask yourself if you've ever done any of the following:

- Ventured out after a hard, tiring day at the office for the fun of joining your mates in the pub
- Spent hours packing, preparing and queuing in crowded airports for a long-awaited, much-anticipated holiday
- Braved the cold, wind and snow to get to the corner shop for a bar of chocolate in the middle of a freezing winter's night

You have? Then read my lips: you're not lazy.

<u>What Procrastination *Is*</u>

That's what procrastination isn't. So what is it? Put simply, it's a particularly cunning form of inner obstacle. *It arises when our desire to act is overwhelmed by an equal or stronger desire to stay still.* Its job is to protect us and to keep us from blundering off into the dangerous unknown. We may not be consciously aware of this other, opposing desire, but the effect is always the same – immobility.

<u>Why Procrastination Appears</u>

Procrastination takes many forms and appears for a variety of reasons. Here are just some of them:

- **You're demotivated** (see above)

- **You're tired and genuinely need a rest**. Perhaps you really do just want (and need) to chill out and relax before you get on with chasing your dreams or doing your chores. If your body is shouting "Enough!" and your primitive mind is listening, it'll send procrastination out as the cavalry to rescue you from further discomfort and exhaustion. The problem is that this respite is only ever a temporary one and is even more tiring in the long-term because you're left with the undone task still on your to-do list.

- **You have a distorted view of time**. If you repeatedly tell yourself, "I'll do it tomorrow, it'll be easier then," you've fallen into the trap of believing that tomorrow ever comes. It doesn't. Haven't you noticed? By the time it arrives, it's today and you're back to thinking, "I'll do it tomorrow." It's that vicious cycle that's so difficult to break out of. Also, you may mistakenly be viewing tomorrow as a blank slate, full of promise, potential and free time. Again, this is a misperception. When tomorrow arrives and becomes today, it will be as full of all of the same obligations and annoyances as any other day.

That's not to say that some days aren't more suitable for doing certain tasks than others. But we're not talking about the sensible scheduling of tasks here; we're talking about your resistance tricking you into putting things off until another day, with the result that you just stay stuck. To quote an old Spanish proverb: "Tomorrow is always the busiest day of the week."

- **You're working (or playing) without limits**. In our society, we tend to think of limits as restrictions which curtail our freedom. Yet, ascribing limits to your life and workload can be one of the most liberating things you'll ever do. Defining limits for any task at hand can make it far less daunting and therefore, considerably more manageable. Artists and writers instinctively understand this, which is why some of our greatest works of literature appear in some clearly defined forms – consider plays, poems, and marble sculptures.

Without limits (an example of a limit would be curtailing the number of hours you spend on a task), you're left with endless choices and a diffuse focus. You don't know where you'll finish, so it's hard to get started. *With* limits, you can exercise freedom within boundaries, and with the end in sight, you may feel far more inclined to get going in the first place.

- **You're afraid.** In my experience, both personally and in my work with clients, this is the single most common reason that procrastination occurs. You don't have to be rigid with terror to become immobilised by procrastination. It can be far more subtle than that. Fear always has one of two roots: either you believe you *won't get something you want* (the results you were aiming for, the joy you believed the activity would bring you, the praise and respect you craved) or that you're *going to lose something you already have* (free time, recognition, your sense of potential, other options).

  Of course, this is the major reason procrastination appears when we're trying to do something that means a lot to us. The danger level appears high and because we have a lot to gain, we feel we have a lot to lose, so we stay put rather than take the risk. This may not be consciously in our awareness until we look more closely at how we're feeling.

So, what to do? Like all forms of inner obstacle, the best approach to procrastination is to figure out what it's telling you and then work your way around it.

Strategies for Tackling Procrastination

The solution to your procrastination will depend on the cause of it. However, each of the techniques that follow employs some combination of dealing with fear, managing time, creating limits and becoming aware of your feelings. These are the procrastination busters I've found to be most effective in my own life and in my work with coaching clients and workshop participants.

- **1. Don't Go Cold Turkey.** First of all, don't ever fall into the trap of telling yourself you'll never procrastinate again. Sorry to be the bearer of bad tidings, but you will. This is because there is an upside to procrastination. It can carve out some much-needed downtime for you, especially when you haven't done so for yourself.

We all need downtime. That's why making commitments like "I'll never procrastinate again" won't work and are actually dangerous, because you'll be left feeling terrible when procrastination reappears. In fact, you may find yourself procrastinating even more because you've just added extra pressure and very effectively awakened your own inner resistance. You can minimise the likelihood of it appearing by scheduling your downtime, rather than letting *it* schedule *you*.

2. **Create a Goofing-off Timetable**. This one is all about planning your avoidance patterns into your daily life. The simplest way is to block out some relaxation time in your diary – a bit like free periods in school – and mark these out as being distinct from the times when you're working on a specific personal or work-related project. Then make sure when the free periods come round, you actually *do* goof off and do the fun stuff that you love doing.

   That might not work, however, if you're like me and don't always obey your own instructions. In this case, you need to carefully consider your personal work/reward preferences. Do you like to work first and then have fun, or have fun first and then get down to work? (I'm using "work" here in the widest sense: not just your day job, but any activity that isn't pure relaxation, including doing your chores and following the exercises in this book).

   Once you know what your preference is, go through your diary and block out some "you" time. That is, time that's related to your own commitments as opposed to other people's (like your family's). Once you've found these blocks of time, split them into two. Then you have a choice: if you like to play first, and can trust yourself to stop playing and start working when the time is up, you get to goof-off for the first half of the period. Then it's down to business. If you prefer to work first then play, it goes the other way round.

   It's *essential* that you obey the equal split, at least at first. The time will come when you'll find yourself wanting more of that precious time for working on your cherished projects, but until that time comes, be strict with yourself – don't curtail your goofing-off time.

How does this work? Simply because structured downtime is far more energising than accidental downtime that comes laden with guilt and frustration (which is how it comes in the package labelled "procrastination"). Think of how differently you feel after you've consciously decided to put your feet up and watch a great DVD, compared to how you feel after mindlessly slumping in front of the TV watching nothing in particular and then discovering that several hours have passed. With this conscious approach, you'll feel better and find that procrastination loosens its grip.

3. **The "First Action" Approach.** One of the most galling things about procrastination is that we often find that the thing we were putting off can be done very quickly and easily once we get started. Yet, as we have seen, getting started can be incredibly difficult. This technique allows you to fool the primitive part of your mind into thinking you aren't actually going to do the task at all – just some tiny part of it – and so the resistance to the task gets switched off. It's a variation on the "smallest unit of gain" idea I described in the section on demotivation.

If you're faced with writing an essay, for example, you might be daunted about the task of "writing an essay". However, you might find the idea of "opening a Word document and typing the essay question and title" entirely achievable. So that's what you do; you say to yourself, "I'm not going to write the essay just now. I'm just going to open a Word document and type the essay question and title." That's it. You've taken the first action, and you might find that that first action is enough to propel you into further action. When I was at university, many an essay I was fretting about got written this way.

The technique can be applied to any task. Making a phone call you've been postponing could start with "looking up the number and writing it down on a piece of paper by the phone". Decorating a wall could start with "opening the can of paint and dipping a brush into it". Cleaning the inside of your car could start with "getting the vacuum cleaner out of the cupboard".

You could apply this to any of the exercises in this book. You could also apply it to filling in a job application, or writing the business plan for your first business venture.

The important thing is to give yourself permission to stop after the first action. In fact, if it's all you feel like doing, you *must* stop. Remember, we're trying to keep you feeling safe so that your slumbering resistance doesn't start waking up. Even if you don't do any more of the task, you've made a start. Best of all, however, you may find that the next action after that ("writing an essay plan", "dialling the number", "dabbing paint on the wall", "plugging the vacuum cleaner into the socket") follows on quite naturally and before you know it, you're up and running and the task is nearly done.

4. **Work in Bursts (With a Cast-Iron Get-Out Clause).** With this technique, you limit yourself to timed bursts of activity. Instead of saying, "I'm going to clean the entire inside of my car," you commit to doing 5 minutes of the activity (or 10 or 15 – whatever works for you), with the option of stopping after any of the timed bursts. So, set a timer, do 5 minutes of cleaning then decide if you want to do another 5 or you would rather stop. Either choice is fine.

    The guarantee of being able to stop is what keeps you feeling safe, but you may find you want to do another 5 minutes. You may find that you'll be able to do several bursts of 5 or 10 or 15 minutes, and then want to stop. You may find you get the whole thing done. Whatever happens, you'll still have done more than you would have had you never started, and that fact alone can make getting the task finished that much easier in the long run.

5. **Define Your Limits.** As I mentioned above, defining boundaries actually generates, rather than depletes, your freedom. If you're resisting doing something, it may be because, on some level, you're seeing the task at hand as having no end. If you're able to set a specific cap on it ("today, I'll just mow the front lawn, as opposed to the front, back and side") you'll probably find it much easier to get started, particularly if you're using techniques 4 and 5 as well. This applies to taking breaks, too.

Not only are you much more efficient when you take proper, regular breaks, you'll find that these breaks create ready-made limits and boundaries which enable you to "chunk" your tasks into manageable segments.

6. **Leave Yourself Wanting More.** Many people find it hard to pick a task up again after they've had a break from it. They've beaten procrastination and got started, only to find the beast comes back again as strong as ever the next time they try to pick up that same task. This is because we have a tendency to stop working at a natural breaking-off point. For example, we may stop painting and take a break after we've finished an entire wall, or we may take a break from essay-writing when we've finished a particular paragraph or page. Consequently, starting again feels like starting something new.

If you can break this sense of newness, you'll find starting up again much easier. So, if you have a break when you've painted just half a wall, when you come back to it you won't be starting out again on a fresh wall, you'll be finishing off the old one. Since procrastination most often strikes when we're about to *start* something, this is a cunning way of thwarting it. As human beings, we tend to gravitate towards a sense of completion and will work for that from wherever we are. Breaking off mid-task (rather than at a natural break point) creates a sense of incompletion which we'll want to resolve.

You can apply this principle to lots of things: mowing the lawn (take a break after mowing half the lawn), reading a book (stop reading in the middle of a chapter), writing an essay (stop writing mid-sentence), filling in a job application (take a break half way through a question). Leave yourself wanting more so that the sense of completion only really comes when you have completed the entire task. Some people may not like this approach because it delays the gratification of finishing discrete parts of the work. Remember, however, this is about outsmarting procrastination, and believe me – it works.

Procrastination is something best put off
until tomorrow.

~ Gerald Vaughan

Blockbuster Strategy 3:
Facing Up to Your False Assumptions

It's not uncommon to feel stuck because you're labouring under false assumptions about what's possible for you. These assumptions can be things you've heard from other people, or that seem to have been "proven" by past experiences. But the truth is that many of them are myths that need to be cleared up before you can move on.

Here's a summary of some of the most common assumptions I find my clients wrestling with, and the truths that lie behind them:

Assumption: "I need everything (including me) to be perfect before I begin looking for my ideal work."

Truth: In reality, things are neither perfect nor imperfect. They just are. If you're caught in this kind of thinking, you're dealing with a security issue. You want to be sure that what you're striving for is going to work out and until you feel you're on a firm footing, you're unwilling to set out. But that kind of certainty just doesn't exist and we don't need it to. The only way you can gather all the information you're going to need to be able to achieve your goals is to start moving before you know how things will work out. It'll bring you into contact with opportunities and with other people. Forget perfection and get going!

Assumption: "I'm too shy to work at my dream job."

Truth: This barrier tends to pop up when you believe that the thing you want is going to require you to be someone you're not. Bear this in mind: you don't have to do anything that's too far out of your comfort zone. Start small and watch your confidence grow. You don't have to move straight from your comfort zone into a terror zone. You just need to stretch yourself, step by step, and you'll be able to make the transition at your own pace. Carrying out a dress rehearsal (see Chapter 7) can help you to overcome this assumption, because it enables you to test the waters before you plunge in.

Also, bear in mind that the whole premise of this book is that you build your Vital Vocation around your own brand of talents, values, environmental considerations, and favourite skills. You're going to find that your Vital Vocation is something that fits you like a glove.

Assumption: "If I'm too successful, I'll alienate the people I love."

Truth: Are there people around you now who are unhappy with their lot? If so, you might be shying away from being all you can be, because you fear making them feel worse, or perhaps you're picking up on their fears that you are moving away from them. Bear in mind that you don't have to change yourself to change your life – you're always going to be you whatever job you find yourself in.

Also, making yourself smaller isn't going to make anyone else bigger. To get yourself out of this bind, you may need to reassure the people you love that they're just as important to you as they always were. You may also need to reassure yourself of this. Be prepared to invest some quality time in your important relationships, but be careful that they don't hold you back from doing what you want to do.

Assumption: "I'm hopelessly under-qualified to do this job; I'm only good at one thing."

It sometimes seems that successful people have a multitude of talents, doesn't it? However, it's more likely that they're good at one or two things and have focused on those, whilst borrowing or hiring other people to do the stuff they don't like. You could do the same. If you're only really good at one thing then you're a specialist and that can be a great thing to be. Go all out to become an expert in your field and find ways of enlisting help from others to handle the things you're not so good at. Some jobs come ready-made with this kind of support.

If you're a manager, you're likely to have staff with a range of abilities, so you don't need to be an expert in everything. If you feel you really do need to build your skills and knowledge in a particular area, don't be afraid to invest in the future through additional education and training (if you're currently employed, you may find your employer can help towards the costs of this – or even cover the costs entirely).

Assumption: *"I can't settle on just one thing for a career because I keep changing my mind!"*

Truth: Do you worry that you want too many things or that you're terminally indecisive? If so, it's possible that you're in very good company with others throughout history who've enjoyed a multitude of talents and who found ways of pursuing them all (think of Leonardo Da Vinci or Benjamin Franklin). If you genuinely love and are interested in lots of things then you're a "renaissance soul". The solution for you isn't to force yourself to specialise, but to find ways of doing at least some parts of everything you love.

If you think this describes you, there are some good books on the subject of how to pursue all your interests. A good place to start is in Michael Gelb's How *to Think Like Leonardo Da Vinci*, and (my particular favourite) *Refuse To Choose* by Barbara Sher.

Assumption: *"I can't find my Vital Vocation because I can't afford to give up my current job."*

Truth: Who said you had to give up your current job in order to pursue a new one? Not me. Go back and read the beginning of this book. Provided you're in a job that leaves you with enough time to have a life outside of work, and which doesn't stress you out so much that you can't think of anything else, then there's no problem. Use your free time to do at least a little bit of what you love. An hour or two a day spent building a home business or studying for a necessary qualification is better than nothing, and a lot more than many people make the time for.

Assumption: "I'll never be able to make a living doing what I love. It's too weird."

Truth: Many people do make a living at unusual things – yes, even in these uncertain times. Almost anything can be turned into a career, if you can find the right niche and the right market. In the online article *37 Weird Jobs You Can Actually Make a Living At* (http://www.jobprofiles.org/library/guidance/weird-jobs.htm) you'll see that people earn their pay at such diverse occupations as: odour testers, hair boilers, crocodile wranglers and ski-slope illustrators. We're quite wrong when we assume that the things we love can't make us a living.

However, that doesn't mean the thing you love *should* make you a living. Some people prefer not to subject their passions to the pressure of making it in a marketplace. Instead, you could find a job that pays the bills and use that to subsidise the pursuit of your heart's desire.

Assumption: "I'm just too negative to get what I want."

Truth: No, you're not, unless your negative thinking has become so chronic and pervasive that it's making you miserable. If you're just generally a "glass-half-empty" person, that's fine. One of the most irritating aspects of the current self-help industry is the fact that it gives the impression that nothing can be achieved in life without "positive thinking". This is not so; bear in mind that so-called negative thinking can be very useful. You can use it to help you find what you want, not by stewing in it, but by developing it in much the same way as you'd develop a photograph from its negative.

Take some time to write down everything you *don't* want and all the ways you're sure you *can't* get what you want. Be specific and detailed. Then, take your lists and flip them round, as we have done in several of the exercises in this book. So, "I *don't want* a job that involves sitting at a desk all day" could become "I *want* a job that requires me to move around between a variety of different outdoor locations". You've started with what you don't want and now the outline of what you do want has become apparent.

Assumption: "It's too much of a leap for me. I'll never make it."

Truth: Do you know exactly what you want, but think it's impossible because it's just so far away from where you are now? Perhaps you've decided you want to be a brain surgeon and you haven't even got a basic school-level science qualification?

There are two ways to deal with a scenario like this. The first is to figure out the steps you need to go through to become qualified as a brain surgeon (e.g. start with that school-level science qualification); the second is to figure out how to get the rewards of being a brain surgeon without actually becoming one. What it is about being a brain surgeon that appeals to you most? Helping people? Doing delicate work with your hands? Learning about human biology? Once you know, you can start to figure out how to get those things, without having to qualify as a brain surgeon. That could mean doing something that's different to what you expected but no less fulfilling.

I know of one woman who bitterly regretted not studying medicine because she decided – quite late in life – that she would have made a good surgeon. By following the process above, she figured out what turned her on most about the idea and found a suitable alternative; she became an assistant in a veterinary surgery, and very happy into the bargain.

If you recognised yourself in any of the above examples, you're probably already beginning to feel a bit more hopeful. Often, simply recognising that we've made a false assumption about what's possible is enough to begin the process of getting unstuck.

Blockbuster Strategy 4: Dealing With Stress

Both job-hunting and work itself (even work you love) can be very stressful. We all know that a degree of stress in life is necessary in order to function effectively, but problems can arise when stress gets out of hand or when our ability to deal with it is compromised through tiredness or illness. It's therefore very important to develop strong coping mechanisms and stress-management skills to help you through the tough times.

I want to share with you a few of my favourite techniques. We'll start with some basics that you can easily incorporate into your daily life ('Your Six-Step Stress-Busting Arsenal'). We'll then go on to consider two very powerful stress-busting techniques. The first ('The Quieting Reflex') can, with practice, become a habit, and be used the moment a stressful situation arises. The other ('The Work') is really useful for dealing with any thoughts which are causing you on-going stress and suffering.

Stress-Busting Technique 1: Your Six Step Stress-Busting Arsenal

Try to incorporate as many of these as possible into your daily life, every day. I've arranged them in order of importance; in other words, you should ensure you're doing number one first, then two, then three and so on. The later options won't work if they're just papering over cracks. Make sure you're giving yourself the benefit of a firm foundation.

1. **Take care of the basics**. Eat well, exercise regularly and get enough sleep.

2. **Don't force yourself to feel positive when you don't**. But do cultivate relationships and regular activities which nurture and support you, and encourage natural positive thoughts. Ditch activities (and people) that encourage the opposite.

3. **Let off steam when you need to**. If tension is building up, talk

to a friend, go for a brisk walk or allow yourself to have a guilt-free temper tantrum (an understanding friend can help by cheering you on as you let off steam). Most of all, don't let your stress or tension build up inside you.

4. **Incorporate stress-reducing techniques into your daily life**. Pick at least one every day and do it. Mindful exercise such as Tai Chi or Yoga, deep breathing and progressive muscle relaxation (using a relaxation CD if necessary) can all be helpful.

5. **Respect your spirit.** You don't have to be religious or in any way mystical to recognise that you have a "spirit" – the part of you that's the true essence of who you are. Nurture it. The Vital Vocation process is about doing that in a *big* way, but build in the smaller ways too: make time every day to do something you really enjoy, no matter how small.

6. **Seek help.** If you're really struggling, don't go it alone. Sometimes professional help from a doctor is what you need (if you're dealing with depression). If you're having a hard time at work, it may be worth speaking to your boss or the personnel department (I'll cover dealing with bullying at work later in the book).

Stress-Busting Technique 2: The Six Second Quieting Reflex

This is a technique to practise using as often as you can. Based on the work of Charles F. Stroebel M.D., it is discussed in detail in his fascinating book by the same name, *The Quieting Reflex* (published by Berkeley Publications but now sadly out of print).

The basic premise is simple: when we are faced with an immediately stressful situation (someone is rude to us, we lose our keys, we're asked to do extra work at the last minute) we are genetically programmed to experience an "alarm response". Our breathing becomes rapid, our heart-rate increases and our muscles tense. This isn't a bad thing; it's evolution's way of ensuring we're able to run or fight, should we need to. This is very handy if a sabre-toothed tiger leaps out at us, but less so in the 21st century when a more measured response would be more helpful. Too much time spent in this "alarm" mode depletes our reserves and leads us towards illness.

How to get around this?

Stroebel's method involves using the first sign of a stressful situation to trigger a "quieting response": a conscious technique of calming our bodies down in the moment that stress is happening. It takes some effort at first and requires consistent practice, but the theory – borne out by research detailed in the book – is that regular use of this technique enables us to cultivate the Quieting Reflex: an *automatic* response which is appropriate to the experience we're having.

In other words, we can "program" ourselves to instantly (and almost unconsciously) recognise when to respond with alarm and when to respond in a more measured way, thus saving us a great deal of tension and anxiety. Stroebel summarises the result as "an alert mind in a calm body".

The technique should be practised whenever a stressful event occurs and also practised consciously at least once a day, even when no stress is happening. In this latter case, imagine yourself in a stressful situation and "mimic" the physical tension you would normally feel before proceeding with the process.

The whole thing should take no more than six seconds. Over a period of time – around six weeks – the response should become automatic in appropriate situations. Here's the drill:

> **Cue**. Notice the signs of stress in the moment: tension, annoyance, anxiety, an alteration in breathing (shallow rapid breaths).

> **Response**. Consciously "smile inwardly" by imagining yourself doing so. Move your eyes and mouth into the position of a smile, even if only slightly. This will automatically trigger a degree of relaxation.

> **Say inwardly to yourself, *"alert mind, calm body."*** This "self-suggestion" will help trigger further relaxation.

> **Take an easy, deep breath.** Don't force it, just consciously do it.

On the exhale, let your jaw, tongue and shoulders go limp; feel a wave of slight heaviness go through your body from top to bottom; feel a wave of slight warmth follow it, from your head right down to your toes.

Resume normal activity.

The Quieting Reflex works well for immediate stress. But what about the chronic stresses and worries that undermine our confidence and lead to a continual sense of unease and suffering? For these, here is another technique which can be very useful.

Stress-Busting Technique 3: The Work of Byron Katie

"The Work" is a process of self-enquiry developed by a woman named Byron Katie. You can read more about her (she has a fascinating history) and the process on her website at www.thework.com. At that site, you can also freely download all the materials you need to do The Work.

The Work involves identifying the thoughts that are causing us stress and limitation, writing them down and putting them up against four questions and what Katie calls a "turnaround". The four questions are:

- **Is it true?**
- **Can you absolutely know that it's true?**
- **What happens when you believe the thought?**
- **Who would you be without the thought?**

Then comes the invitation to turn the thought around to its opposite (each thought often has several opposites) and to find at least three genuine examples of how the turned-around thought could be as true, or even truer, than the original. It's as simple as that, yet the results can be profound.

Here's a brief example of The Work in practice:

- **Stressful thought:** *"I'll never find my dream job."*
- **Question 1: Is it true?** *Yes.* (Katie emphasises that the best

answer to question 1 is either "Yes" or "No": one syllable. A "Yes" is as good as a "No". Be careful not to leave the enquiry by feeling the need to justify your answer).

- **Question 2: Can you absolutely know that it's true that you'll never find your dream job?** *Well, no. I can't absolutely know that, even though I keep thinking it.* (Again, the best answer here is a simple "Yes" or "No").

- **Question 3: How do you react - what happens - when you believe the thought?** *I feel terrible – sad and depressed. I get a heaviness in my chest and a tightness in my throat. My head aches. I start doubting myself, even in my current job. I feel so despondent I stop looking for alternatives. I wonder if it's even worth the bother. I get short-tempered with my partner and my kids. I obsess over things. I feel jealous of other people who seem to be in their dream jobs.*

- **Question 4: Who would you be without the thought?** *Happier. Less stressed. More relaxed and open. I wouldn't be so full of doubt. I'd be willing to try new things and do things that might move me closer to my dream job. I'd feel like I had nothing to lose. I'd be easier to be around.*

- **The turnaround:** *"I will find my dream job."*

- **Examples of why this could be as true or truer:**

  1. *Lots of people do find their dream jobs*

  2. *There's no real reason I can't – I have the ability.*

  3. *If I don't believe the thought, I'll be more willing to try new things.*

  4. *Circumstances could change in my current job and I may be offered something even better.*

The Work is particularly useful for dealing with underlying troublesome thoughts which cause on-going feelings of stress or limitation, but it can be applied to any thought that's troubling you. There are many helpful examples of Katie doing The Work on YouTube, and the entire process is outlined in detail in her excellent book with Stephen Mitchell, *Loving What Is*.

EXERCISE 20: Releasing Your Limitations!

Step 1

For the duration of the next week, use the **Quieting Reflex** process whenever you become aware of stress or tension. Make a note of any results in your journal.

Step 2

Choose a thought that is particularly troubling you at present. It may be a thought that begins "I can't" or "I should" or "He/she/they should". Read the instructions for doing **The Work** and apply the process to the thought. Make a note of how you feel afterwards in your journal.

 Self-Coaching Questions

1. Is there anything going on in other areas of your life that is putting pressure on your ability to properly focus on finding your Vital Vocation? What actions can you take now to address these issues?

2. What is the most compelling reason to move forward in finding your ideal work? Why must this be done?

3. Which aspects of your future career path are under your current control and which aren't? What can you do now about the parts you can change for the better?

PART TWO: GETTING IT

You're not going to see your dreams come true if you don't put wings, legs, arms, hands and feet on 'em.

~ Dolly Parton

CHAPTER 9
LAYING A FIRM FOUNDATION

Do you wish to be great? Then begin by being. Do you desire to construct a vast and lofty fabric? Think first about the foundations of humility. The higher your structure is to be, the deeper must be its foundation.

~ Saint Augustine

If you have built castles in the air, your work need not be lost; that is where they should be. Now put the foundations under them.

~ Henry David Thoreau

Before We Begin

We're about to get very practical indeed. Having spent some time excavating your Vital Vocation, it's now time to take some solid steps towards finding or creating it in the outside world.

At this point, it's entirely possible that your initial enthusiasm is giving way to a sense of unease.

Are you worrying about the condition of the job market? Or that you'll be too scared to take a leap from a secure (but unsatisfactory) job into something new? Maybe you worry that, despite your enthusiasm for a radical change, the people around you – including people who depend on you – won't be quite so positive that it's a good idea.

All of this is absolutely fine and completely natural. But we're not going to let it derail you. You might be worrying that you can't, but believe me – you can.

And guess what? You don't have to succumb to the economic crisis or take any unnecessary risks or upset the people you love in order to do the work of your dreams. If you're still troubled by niggling feelings of doubt, remind yourself of how to tackle such internal obstacles by reviewing the contents of Chapter 8. In Chapters 10 and 11, we're going to look at how you can tackle any external real-world obstacles that come up. *This* chapter, however is about getting ready for the part of the journey that's about actually going after what you really want.

First, we're going to lay some firm foundations for you so that you can get off to a really strong start.

How to Beat the Recession

If you're like most of the job-hunting, career-changing population, concerns about money will be close to the top of your list of worries. I can't wave a magic wand and make all your money woes disappear, but I do have a couple of helpful techniques to help quell the worst of your financial fears.

In this section, we'll take a look at how and why you can beat the recession and also some first-aid for fear – for when you're suddenly out of work and feel panicked. Finally, we'll close with a look at how you can get your finances onto a surer footing.

Why There's Still Hope, Even in the Toughest of Times

Worries about the effect of the economic downturn are probably the most prevalent of all those that currently plague job-seekers, career-changers and new business-builders. These fears are not entirely unfounded. There is no doubt that the recession has had an appalling effect on many industries, communities, families and individuals. I'm well aware that many of you reading this will have been affected, perhaps through the loss of a job, or through a significant reduction in income.

If you have just lost your job and are in a state of panic about what to do, move to the section below called *First Aid For Emergency Career Disasters*. This outlines some immediate steps you can take to deal with the position you're in. Take those steps then come back here and resume reading.

Without wishing to dismiss the seriousness of the situation the recession puts us all in, I want to emphasise something that's really important to understand:

> *There are jobs out there. There are always jobs out there and there are always new jobs being created.*

This isn't wishful thinking; it's simple logic. Even if no new jobs were being created, employees in existing jobs would still get sick, die, retire, take long sabbaticals, win the lottery and leave, decide to move abroad, or start working part-time.

In addition to that, many organisations - forced to change their shape to cope with a radically different financial environment - will restructure and in the process, create new jobs. In other words, vacancies *will* arise. The trick is to discover the appropriate vacancies (or gaps in the market, if you're an entrepreneur) and out of all the people who are seeking work or looking for business opportunities, put yourself in the best position to fill the gap.

It's also true to say that, even in boom times, there are *always* people falling out of work. So the recession doesn't mean that you have to deal with an entirely different job market to the norm, but it does mean that you have to deal with one that's operating on an entirely different scale.

The solution? There isn't one – not in the sense of you being able to "solve" the problem of the recession. Time will do that and in the meantime, what do *you* do? Firstly, you deal with your immediate situation – financially, emotionally and psychologically. Then, you do what this book has been specifically designed to help you with: you sharpen your job-hunting skills to a finely-honed point and you enact a practical, tactical job-search or career-change process.

If you haven't done so already, please go to my website at <u>www.</u>

cormackcarr.com and download my free eBook *The Top 10 Best and Worst Ways to Find a New Job*. This will equip you with some immediate information on the best job-hunting techniques out there. It covers:

- Sending your CV to prospective employers vs. using your personal networks to help you find work.

- Using the internet vs. making an untargeted personal approach to employers.

- Answering job adverts in the press vs. a targeted personal approach to employers.

- Using employment agencies vs. using job-hunt clubs.

- Undertaking a strategic job search using a programme such as the one outlined in this book.

First Aid for Emergency Career Disasters

If you've just lost your job unexpectedly, chances are that you're feeling pretty low. Your first instinct may be to think "why me?" especially if there are others in your workplace who weren't similarly affected.

Although you may realise that many people look back on unplanned redundancies as useful turning points in life that led them to bigger and better things, that's small comfort if you're facing the loss of a regular income and still have commitments to keep.

Take a deep breath, sit down with a pen and your Vital Vocation Journal and start making some notes. In seven steps, you can be back in control. Your immediate job is to find a new job; go at it with real commitment to yourself, as though you were your own boss!

Seven-Step Emergency Job-Loss Action Plan

1. **Don't panic.** Easy to say, I know, but you're about to sort out what to do, step-by-step. Take your time over this and you'll feel much better at the end of it. *For ongoing stress-relief, refer back to Chapter 8.*

2. **Consider your immediate priorities**. For most people, this will relate to their finances. Unless you have a nest-egg which

enables you to survive comfortably without work for a few weeks, you'll need to:

- Maximise your income
- Minimise your outgoings

Write both of these points as a heading in your journal and start writing ideas under each. Under "Maximise Your Income" you might write: "sell stuff on eBay", "apply for relevant benefits", "cash-in my investments". Under minimise your outgoings you might write: "take a mortgage holiday", "move into shared accommodation"; "search for budget deals on the internet".

For each of the possible actions you've written, make a note of one thing you'd need to do next in order to move that action forward and a date by which you'll do it. For example, if you want to apply for benefits, but aren't sure what you're entitled to (and you're a UK resident), you may write "Contact local Citizens Advice Bureau (www.citizensadvice.org.uk) for information – Monday at 9am".

If you live in America, you might want to investigate options such as Welfare Programmes (www.welfareinfo.org) and eligibility for Nutrition Assistance (www.fns.usda.gov/fns). Take your time over this step and try to include as many "next actions" – with deadlines – as possible. You'll feel much better for knowing you're doing something practical about your situation. ***For more help to get your finances on a sure footing, see Exercise 21, below.***

3. **Take a self-inventory**. An earlier part of this programme is about doing this in much greater detail, but as an immediate action, make a note in your journal of all the skills you have and all the qualities you know you possess which will be attractive to future employers.

   Try to stretch your imagination here. Don't just write down skills you've used previously in work. Also write down skills you know you have but which you haven't yet had a chance to use in work. For example, can you drive? You may not have driven as part of your job but, nonetheless, if you've passed your driving test, that's a skill that can definitely be used in the workplace.

Also write down what general things you might consider doing now that you're not tied to your job. Examples might include doing temp work, applying for part-time jobs, volunteering until you find work, going freelance or going into business with other ex-colleagues. *For more information on taking a Skills Inventory, refer back to Chapter 5.*

4. **Update your Curriculum Vitae.** Sending unsolicited CVs to prospective employers isn't a very effective way of finding work unless you tailor your CV to the employer and target employers based on a good fit for your skills. Make sure you at least have a template CV available, however, so you can tweak it when you need it. Take time to think deeply about what to add to it based on any recent learning or work experience.

   Make sure that for each tailored CV you include the information that's most relevant to the employer you're sending it to in the first few lines. Many CVs are only glanced at before they're discarded; you'll greatly increase your chances of making an impact if you think carefully about what to put at the very beginning. *For more information on making an effective CV, see Chapter 12.*

5. **Contacts: Don't burn your bridges!** You may well be feeling very angry that you've lost your job. If you feel you've been genuinely badly treated by your employer, and that you have a case against them, then by all means seek out some good quality legal advice (you can get it free at the Citizens Advice Bureau service in the UK).

   However, if you know you've been treated legally, don't let your initial anger get in the way of keeping some useful contacts warm at your recent place of work. If you can, send a note to your previous employer – perhaps to your manager or the personnel department – saying how much you enjoyed working there and how much you learned from the experience.

   Try to do this as soon as possible after you leave. Be sure to include your up-to-date contact details and an up-to-date CV. It may feel odd to do this so soon after losing your job, but you'll be amazed at the doors it may open for you in the future, particularly when times look brighter for your previous employer.

6. **Contacts: Build some new bridges.** A huge number of job opportunities are encountered through the process of networking. Therefore, it's vitally important when you're out of work not to let yourself become isolated. Make sure you keep up with as many of your old professional contacts as possible and also make an effort to cultivate some new ones.

   Make sure you tell people you're out of work and are actively looking. That includes friends, family, ex-colleagues and even casual acquaintances. You'll be surprised at how many of them will subsequently keep you in mind and will direct you to job opportunities they become aware of. It's useful to prepare what you'll say to someone who asks "What are you doing now?" You don't want to mumble and bluster; you want to be able to say something clear and memorable like, "I'm an advertising executive currently between jobs and looking for a new challenge."

   Don't sound apologetic – sound enthusiastic. *For more information on building a powerful network of support, see Chapter 11.*

7. **Take Action!** Armed with your stabilised finances, your updated CV, your refreshed self-knowledge, your network of contacts and (hopefully) a calmer demeanour, you can start the process of seeking work in earnest.

   In your journal, make a note of the methods that you feel able to immediately concentrate on. Check out *The Best and Worst Ways to Find a New Job* eBook (see above) but bear in mind that if you need to find work quickly for financial reasons, it's always fine to go for a "good enough job" rather than your "ideal career".

   Try to employ a few different job-search methods to maximise your chances. Around four would be an optimum and manageable number. Examples include:

   - Signing up at temping agencies

- Signing up at employment agencies
- Signing up at statutory job services
- Joining pre-existing job-clubs
- Setting up your own job-club (more on this later)
- Looking on the internet and signing up for relevant online job pages
- Sending your (tailored!) CV to relevant prospective employers
- Placing an order for the local jobs newspaper
- Exploring options for retraining.

Getting Your Finances onto a Sure Footing

Whether you're facing imminent unemployment or not, it's always a sensible idea to get your finances under control.

Of course, that's easier said than done! Few things arouse such strong emotions as money matters. When faced with job uncertainty, those emotions are often difficult ones, particularly if you haven't got a great deal of money or are facing the loss of your income. Even if your income is good, you may be in a position – like many of us – of not making the most of that income. Few of us are taught properly about budgeting or investing, and consequently we're left feeling as if we're at the mercy of money rather than feeling that we're in control of it.

We also live in a credit-based society, where it's common to be in considerable debt. It's beyond the scope of this book to go into great detail about how to manage money more effectively, but the exercise below gives some useful pointers.

EXERCISE 21: Your Financial Self-Audit

Step 1

Assess Your Current Financial Situation

- How long could you live your present lifestyle if you stopped working tomorrow? How many weeks' worth of income have you saved for emergencies? (A good rule of thumb for the future: aim to have twelve weeks' worth of income saved for emergency situations).

- What is the value of your assets (e.g. house, car, shares and other financial investments)? How easily could they be turned into cash if you needed some?

- How much is your total debt (e.g. mortgage, personal loans, credit card debts, student loans)? How effective are your repayment plans?

- What is the monthly balance of your income, minus your outgoings?

- How much are you saving every month (savings plans, pensions)?

Step 2

Decide Where You Want to be Financially

- What are your (genuine) financial goals? Do you want lots of money in the future or "just enough"?

- How far away is your desired future at your current income level?

- Have you got a written plan for improving your finances?

Step 3

Educate Yourself

- Invest in a good book on financial management (see the resources section at the end of the book for ideas).

- See an independent financial adviser and discuss your financial situation – and your financial goals – in some detail.

- Learn about investment options that are appropriate to your current needs and your future goals.

- Get real with yourself about some of the questions you have about money and think about where you might find the answers. Don't be afraid to ask!

Step 4

Take Action!

- Start spending less than you earn. This can be hard at first, but it's the only way to start building up a nest egg.

- Analyse your bank statements and identify expenses you can scale back on.

- Think before you buy new things. Ask yourself, do I *really* need this item?

- Automate your savings. Don't fall into the trap of thinking you'll save the money you have left over at the end of the month. If you're like most of us, there won't be any! Start saving at least 10% of your income at the beginning of the month. Put it in a high-interest savings account. Aim to save the equivalent of at least three months' salary for future emergency situations.

- Organise your pension. Old age may seem a long way off, but it doesn't hurt to start saving now. You'll be glad later.

Feeling a bit more stable? From these firmer foundations, let's strike out towards *getting* the Vital Vocation you've worked so hard to uncover.

CHAPTER 10
ACTION PLANNING: Overcoming
External Obstacles Part 1

If you don't design your own plan, chances are you'll fall into someone else's. And guess what they have planned for you? Not much.

~ Jim Rohn

Getting from A to B

So now you have a picture of your Vital Vocation and you've spent some time refining it. You've had a trial run so you know some of the tools that can serve you well on your journey, and you may even have got an early warning of some of the obstacles that are likely to block your way. Now it's time to put everything you've learned, and all the information you've gathered, to work in finding or creating your Vital Vocation. To do that, you need a plan.

I always recommend that my clients take time to put a detailed plan in place for turning the outline of their Vital Vocation into a reality, but I don't kid myself or them that a plan is anything other than a tool to get things moving. It's more fiction than reality but, nonetheless, it's still very useful.

Here's how we usually *plan* to get from point A to point B:

Here's how our path usually looks in *reality*:

Even with a plan, there will no doubt be detours and setbacks, ups, downs, retreats and progress; but creating a plan means that you can have the destination firmly in mind and you can recalibrate as you go. This will help keep things on track (even if the track heads off in unexpected directions) and it will help you to keep moving forward. Some of you will end up exactly where you intended; others will end up somewhere even *better* than you intended; most importantly, those of you who lose your way will be able to quickly find it again.

The action planning process I recommend is one that anyone who works in business or management will be familiar with. It's sometimes called "prior step planning" and here, the business in question is *you*.

The process itself is simple, although you may find that some of the steps you identify can't be carried out immediately or that they seem to throw up seemingly insurmountable obstacles. Don't worry about that now; I have a few tricks for you that will help you get past the real-world obstacles that will inevitably appear in your way.

Firstly, use the following exercise to work out a plan of action of how to get from where you are now to where you want to be.

EXERCISE 22: Prior Step Planning

Step 1

On a clean page in your journal, write a sentence which describes the outcome you're looking for (i.e. your Vital Vocation). Example: "get a job as a primary school teacher."

Step 2

Ask yourself this question: "In order to move forward towards achieving this outcome, what prior step would I have to take first?" Write your answer.

Example:

Outcome: Get a job as a primary school teacher.

What prior step would I have to take first? *Train as a primary school teacher.*

Step 3

Repeat the process for each new statement you write.

Example:

New outcome: Train as a primary school teacher.

What prior step would I have to take first? *Find out about training options.*

New outcome: Find out about training options.

What prior step would I have to take first? *Nothing: I can Google this straight away, or phone the local college tomorrow.*

Step 4

As soon as you get to an action you can carry out *immediately, without having to do something else first*, do it, or make a note of *when* you'll do it. Then make a note of anything else you'll need to do to move forward.

Example:

Action: *Tomorrow morning, I'll make an appointment to visit the nearest teacher training college, which I found through my Google search.*

Step 5

Compile your actions into logical sequence and - as far as is possible - put some timescales against them. If you're unsure of any points, don't worry – you can come back to them later. Just start fleshing out the plan, take note of all the actions you can take immediately and in the short-term, then start taking them!

How to Deal with External Obstacles

The previous exercise may seem simplistic to you, but believe me when I tell you that it's a highly effective and completely essential step. I ensure my coaching clients always complete this exercise *before* they start taking action in the direction of their chosen goal. That way, when they do take action, they have a plan to follow and can therefore get off to a strong start.

Taking action is the only thing that will move you closer to your Vital Vocation. By taking action – almost any action - you'll start making progress, which will be extremely motivating. However, there are two categories of blockage that are likely to come up at some point whenever you take action. The first category is that set of inner obstacles which can root you to the spot. You learned how to deal with those in Chapter 8, so check back there if you need a refresher.

The other category relates to a different type of obstacle altogether – the external obstacle that exists in the real world "out there" rather than inside you. These are obstacles like the financial setback, the recalcitrant boss, the geographical barrier or the qualification you need but don't have. External obstacles sometimes come alone and sometimes in groups.

It's almost certain that you will come up against real-life obstacles on the path to your Vital Vocation. That seems to be part of the deal, so you may as well get ready for it. The good news is that real obstacles – just like internal obstacles – can be got round, or over. And they can sometimes be removed altogether.

There are two broad approaches to dealing with an external obstacle:

1. **You can engage with it directly – that is, change it or remove it.**

2. **You can make it evaporate by changing your perspective on the situation and therefore rendering the obstacle irrelevant.**

Let me give you an example. Let's say you discover that you need to enter training for your new career and then you learn that no training institution near you has any available places, or – worse – that you're too old to be accepted onto the course. Disaster! Or is it?

The first course of action (above) would mean finding a place that offered the training, and – if necessary – travelling there or obtaining the training by distance learning, if that was an option. That might solve the "availability of training" issue, but it might not solve the issue of age limits. That's when a different approach is needed.

This actually happened to Sean, who realised quite late in life that he wanted to train in medicine. He wished he had become a doctor, because he realised his talents lay in the field of caring for people's health, and he had a strong desire to work in a medical/healthcare environment. What he lacked were the skills needed to be a doctor, because he had no training, and at 55 years old he realised that the likelihood of him training in medicine and qualifying as a GP was virtually non-existent.

Far from falling into despondency, he decided to look for ways to express his talent for caring for people's health in other ways; by finding an option that didn't require him to get a medical degree. In the end, he trained as a tai chi instructor (he'd found tai chi to be very beneficial to his own health). He now has his own thriving practice and has even managed to fulfil the "environment" aspect of his Vital Vocation by offering tai chi classes to patients at his local doctor's surgery.

His solution was based on a really important principle that I teach all my clients:

> *You can always have the core of what you love, even if the form it takes isn't what you first anticipated.*

What he really wanted was to help people and by being open-minded enough to realise there were more ways to do this than he first thought, he opened up a world of opportunities.

So, bear in mind that there are always at least two ways of dealing with an obstacle. If where you are is "A", where you want to get to is "B" and your obstacle is "X", there are two questions you must ask yourself:

1. **How can I get from A to B by *directly dealing with or removing* X?**

2. **How can I get from A to B *without having to deal with X*, perhaps by finding another way of getting the kind of fulfilment that I think B would give me?**

These are deceptively powerful questions and they can be applied to any obstacle you face. As you can see from the example above, it's *always* worth looking at your prospective goal in the broadest possible terms. This gives you more options. "Caring for the health of others" makes many more options available to you than "becoming a doctor". Don't tie yourself down too soon. Whenever you're faced with an external obstacle, apply the two questions above.

Block-Busting Self-Coaching Process

You may find it helpful to work through the following process in order to generate new options for yourself whenever you're faced with an obstacle in your path. You might like to think of this process as "self-coaching questions with bells on"!

1. **What is the obstacle?** Try to define it as clearly as possible. Be descriptive of its characteristics. Is it big or small? Permanent or temporary? A minor inconvenience or a mind-numbingly scary brick wall?

2. **Why is it important?** Take time to reflect on exactly why it's an obstacle for you. Is it because it blocks an essential part on your path? Or is it something that you lack, but need to have if you're going to move forward?

3. **What solutions have you already thought of?** It's quite possible that you've already had some ideas about how to work through this obstacle. You may be surprised to discover more when you stop to think! Write them down – even if they seem unrealistic at this stage.

4. **Ask yourself:** *"How can I get from A to B by directly dealing with or removing X?"* To generate ideas, consider:

   - What have you tried so far?

   - Of what you've tried so far, what parts worked (if any) and what does that tell you?

   - Of what you've tried so far, what parts didn't work (if any) and what does that tell you?

   - What likely options haven't you tried yet?

   - What *un*likely options haven't you tried yet? (Be inventive!)

   - Think of the most resourceful person you know (this can be a real person, a celebrity, or a fictional character). In this situation, what would they do? What does that tell you about what you could do?

   - What help can other people give you with this problem?

5. **Ask yourself:** *"How can I get from A to B without having to deal with X, perhaps by finding another way of getting the kind of fulfilment that I think B would give me?"* To generate ideas, consider:

- What is it you love most about the goal you've chosen? Be specific. How will achieving that goal make you feel? How will it make others feel? What difference will it make to you, to your loved ones, to your community, to the world?

- What other options are available to you in terms of getting the same – or a similar – sense of fulfilment?

- What action can you take towards this revised goal?

- What help can other people give you with this problem?

Sometimes, obstacles that we think are insurmountable are actually only temporary setbacks. I have a friend who harboured a keen desire to teach children, but she didn't do anything about it for years because she believed she needed a teaching qualification and had no time to study for one. Then, she was offered an opportunity to do some part-time voluntary work as a teaching assistant (using skills she had developed in her existing day job). Without any idea of anything further coming from it, she took the opportunity. That led – several months later – to an offer of a part-time paid teaching assistant job which she accepted.

By that point, her long-shelved dream of becoming a teacher suddenly seemed attainable again. She used the free time she gained through having a part-time job to study for her teaching qualification. In other words, she started teaching kids (and loving it) long before she qualified as a teacher. By doing something to fulfil herself, she ultimately landed a job that she had long given up on.

Don't Be an Island

You'll notice that as part of my instructions for parts 4 and 5 of the *Block-Busting Self-Coaching Process,* I suggest that you ask other people for help and ideas.

Seeking help is perhaps *the* most powerful thing you can do when you get stuck. In fact, it's so important that I've devoted a whole chapter to it, and that's next.

CHAPTER 11
GETTING SUPPORT:
Overcoming External Obstacles Part 2

If everyone is moving forward together, then success takes care of itself.

~ *Henry Ford*

The Importance of a Support System

Nothing beats getting help from others when you have an obstacle to face. Not only can other people help you generate options for dealing with an obstacle, they can also help you through the process of breaking through it, by cheering you up and egging you on as you move forward.

A great technique shared by the American career counsellor Barbara Sher, author of *It's Only Too Late If You Don't Start Now – How to Create Your Second Life at Any Age,* involves using a sentence which is almost magical in its block-busting ability.

How to Ask for Help: Barbara Sher's Wish/Obstacle Sentence

Its success rests on the fact that most people a) love to help others and b) love to solve problems. It's called the "Wish/Obstacle Sentence".

You'll see that it's similar to the "two types of obstacle" principle described in Chapter 10. Here, instead of trying to figure out how to get past an obstacle all by yourself, you enlist the help of others in a way that actively engages them in helping to solve your problem.

When you want to get from where you are now (point A) to your goal (point B) and are faced with an obstacle (X), you can enlist other people's support by saying:

"I want (to get to) B, but I can't because of X"

For example:

- "I want to become a teacher but I can't because I don't have time to get the qualification I need."
- "I want to make a living as a photographer, but I can't afford a decent camera."
- "I want to work abroad but I don't speak any foreign languages."
- "I want to work only in term-time but I don't know what jobs to go for other than teaching jobs – and I don't want to teach."

If you choose people with open, creative minds (don't pick your gloomiest acquaintances!) you may be surprised at the options they come up with for you. The trick is to *never* reject a suggestion without really considering it deeply first. Even if it seems odd at first, there may be some merit in it.

I used this technique several years ago when I was trying to publicise a new debt-counselling service for the charity I managed at the time. We had virtually no budget for promotion, but needed to let people know about the service. I contacted a trusted colleague and said, "I want to publicise this new service but I can't because I have no promotional budget." His suggestion? "Chain yourself naked to the railings of your building in protest at the country's debt crisis, so you make the evening news."

Great, I thought – some help! The service would certainly get some profile, and I'd probably get arrested. Then I realised that the idea wasn't so bad after all. My staff and I staged a fake "demonstration" outside the building, holding placards saying, "Down With Debt!" and publicising the service by handing out leaflets with details of how people could get free impartial help to deal with their debt.

It wasn't a real demonstration, of course - and no nudity was involved. However, we were able to invite the local paper who came and took pictures and ran an article, giving us much more publicity. Which just goes to show: even the oddest ideas can come with a kernel of usefulness.

Why You Should Build Your Vital Vocation Dream Team

Another highly effective way to help you move forward and deal with obstacles is to surround yourself with a "dream team" of people who are helping you to find your Vital Vocation.

As we grow, we're taught how to make it on our own and to prize our independence. That's a sign of growing up. However, many of us get stuck there and we fail to realise that there's a stage that exists *beyond* independence and it's a very fulfilling place from which to live.

It's called *interdependence*, the point where we recognise and celebrate the fact that we are all parts of a greater whole and that we all can – and do – nurture each other's lives in countless ways. If you want to really take your dreams to the next level, you need to get other people involved in them.

The reason for that is simple. You can guarantee that other people will have the information you lack, the contacts you need, the support you crave and a whole host of great ideas you'd never think of on your own. Have you ever noticed that you often feel better, and lighter, after you've discussed a problem with a good and trusted friend – even when it's a problem you were convinced would be impossible to solve? "I'd never have thought of that!" you say when they offer a great suggestion for a way forward.

The insight that you are blind to (probably because you're feeling scared) will seem obvious to them from their vantage point, and when they see it and tell you about it, you'll see it too. You've probably experienced it from the other side of the fence also – when you can spot an obvious course of action that a friend in trouble is simply missing.

It seems to be a fact of human nature that we often have better and more courageous ideas on behalf of other people than we have for ourselves. It's all to do with how invested we are in a particular outcome and perhaps because it's easier to be brave when you're not the one in the hot seat. For whatever reason, it holds true and it's a useful thing to remind yourself of when you're actively looking for ways to move things forward. There's no question about it – teamwork works.

Here are some key reasons why you should make support from others a key part of your Vital Vocation-finding arsenal:

1. **Other people's assets can help you realise your dream.** One of the greatest advantages to having a team around you is that it enables you to tap into a whole bunch of additional capabilities, including necessary talents and skills that you lack. Also, if you don't have to, you shouldn't be doing the things you're not good at and don't enjoy; not when someone else could do them more productively on your behalf.

   Recently, my client Jason was in the process of setting up a complementary therapy practice and told me he was daunted by the prospect of doing all the financial stuff that setting up the business would entail. He was worried he'd make mistakes because he wasn't confident with numbers.

   My response? *Don't do it.* That's why other people were invented. Ask a friend who loves figures to help out or hire an accountant who enjoys their work (why deprive someone else of the chance to do something they love doing?). That approach can free you up to use your own talents to their full effect, rather than diluting them with tasks that you won't do very well anyway. In my day job, I make a point of hiring talented people whose skills complement my own, because I know they'll do a far better job in certain areas than I ever could.

   He followed that advice and found and hired someone who loves accountancy, while he gets on with doing what he's good at – delivering complementary therapies to his clients.

   If you're worried about money, think of it as an investment, rather than an expense. Having someone else do the stuff you'd prefer not to do can save you money in the long run. You can hire people quickly and at a variety of rates online through sites like www.elance.com or www.odesk.com. It's worth browsing sites like that just to get some idea of the kind of things other people can help you with.

2. **Networking and new contacts can provide vital information.** I've already said that one of the most important reasons to get into action, even if you're unclear of exactly where you're going, is that it gets you up off your backside and out into the world where you can start bumping into people and opportunities. New acquaintances may be able to help you directly or they can put you in touch with other people who can support you.

Perhaps you'll find someone who's happy to give you some useful materials once they know what you're trying to achieve.

Recently, a friend was given an entire set of second-hand language tapes by someone she'd only just met, because she happened to mention at a meeting that she wanted to learn Spanish but was struggling to find a local class that worked with her schedule.

Once you've identified other people who share your passion, or who have a particular set of skills you require, put yourself amongst them and start talking. As well as networking online, network in person by going to discussion groups, speaking events and networking meetings in the areas that interest you.

Details of many of them can be found online (at sites such as www.findnetworkingevents.com) or if your area of passion has a newsletter or magazine associated with it, they'll be advertised in there.

3. **Others will create the accountability that keeps you on track.** Perhaps the most important contribution a Vital Vocation Dream Team can make is in helping you keep to your commitments. Accountability is a vastly underrated part of reaching your goals. How have you ever achieved anything in your life, particularly when the going got tough? With support I hope, but my guess is you did it because you also had someone breathing down your neck, whether that was your parents, a school teacher, the tax man or your boss.

It's difficult to achieve this kind of disciplined accountability alone, since we're subject to so many competing demands and distractions. If you're like me, you may have absolutely no problem in committing to something (for example, completing a course of study by a certain date) and putting it – in bold ink – on your calendar. However, left to your own devices, you may find that date slipping … and slipping … and slipping. If you know that someone else is going to care that you'll do what you've said you'll do, and will be waiting there for you to confirm that you've done it, believe me, you'll move heaven and earth to hit your target. In a dream team, you'll also have someone there to give you a great big cheer when you reach your goal.

You can create an environment of accountability and support simply by asking a friend to "buddy" you in your endeavours – which is why so many people go jogging in pairs – or you could do what successful athletes have been doing for years, and hire a coach (this is the single biggest reason my clients seek me out). A really good coach will work with you to determine the particular blend of accountability and support that will work for you.

How to Build Your Vital Vocation Dream Team

Helping people over obstacles seems to be in our genetic make-up. People love to give advice, don't they? It's important, however, to make sure that the help people offer you is welcome and useful. The trick to getting good advice is to train people to give you good advice.

How? By asking the right questions. Unfortunately, asking for help is something many of us are not good at (try telling a lost driver to ask for directions, if you don't believe me). Try this four-step process to make things easier:

1. **Pick the right people**. Not nice-but-insincere people who'll just say what they think you want to hear, and no hyper-critical people who'll take pleasure in bursting your bubble. You want constructive, supportive people who'll actively look for ways forward for you and who'll feel confident in suggesting ways to

dismantle the barriers you face.

2. **Ask them for help.** The power of asking is an amazing thing. Exactly how you do this depends on the circumstances you and the other person (or persons) are in. If you have friends you trust, ask them for help directly. But when it comes to ideas, the more the merrier, so if you're a member of a social networking site (such as Twitter) or an online discussion board, post your dream and the obstacles you face in achieving it, and just watch the responses come in.

When I was in the process of investigating the benefits of a real food diet, and the materials I might need to incorporate more real food recipes into my life, I asked for advice on an online health and fitness forum I had joined previously at www. ning.com. I was instantly supplied with useful links, contacts, equipment reviews and recipes. I also used social media to "crowdsource" opinions on the best cover this book. That's why it has the cover that it does – because the vast majority of people who responded (and there were many) loved the elephant!

Of course, you don't have to crowdsource online; you could host a dinner party for a group of positive, helpful people and use it as a forum for helping each other, with everyone getting the chance to share their goal and obstacles so that the others can brainstorm solutions.

3. **Think about how you ask for help.** The trick here is to be clear about what you want to achieve and be specific about what's stopping you, but don't overwhelm your dream team by loading them with a laundry list of problems. It's probably best to start with one obstacle first. Once you and the team have solved that, you can move on to something tougher.

4. **Get on-going support.** Once you've seen the value of the input of other human beings, you may want to make that level of support on-going, and this is where creating a longer-term Vital Vocation Dream Team comes in. This is a group that meets regularly, perhaps weekly or fortnightly or monthly, and whose sole purpose is to help make its members' dreams come true. It's a terrific way of creating a powerful environment of support. People will love to come together for the express

purpose of helping you reach your goals – especially if it helps them to reach their own in the process.

Bullying and Harassment: Two Particularly Unpleasant Obstacles

Dealing with a difficult working situation in your current job can often derail you from your efforts to move onto something better. It's a hard situation to be in and a classic "chicken and egg" scenario: you desperately want to make progress, but your daily working environment is sapping your energy and motivation, so you just can't seem to get started in making the change, even though you know that you must if you're ever going to see an improvement.

Two of the most insidious issues many of us will face in our jobs are workplace bullying and harassment. Before we delve into the details, the key thing to remember is that there are always options available which can help you to cope with a situation (if it's annoying but tolerable) or to move yourself out of a situation (if it's really bad). Don't lose heart.

These obstacles are, sadly, fairly common occurrences in a number of workplaces. "Bullying" is when someone tries to intimidate another worker, often in front of colleagues. It is usually, though not always, done to someone in a less senior position. "Harassment" is where someone's behaviour is offensive (for example, making inappropriate sexual comments or abusing someone's race, religion or sexual orientation).

It can sometimes *appear* that you are being bullied when in fact you're not. For example, organisational restructures often lead to an increased workload, and this can sometimes feel like unfair pressure coming from your boss. If you *are* being bullied, and feel able, you could speak directly to the person you suspect is bullying you. This may clarify things one way or the other and – if the person *was* bullying you, intentionally or otherwise – it may shock them enough to stop them in their tracks.

If bullying or harassment persists (or is intentional) you need to get help. You absolutely *do not* need to put up with this behaviour. You can seek help from your employer, perhaps by using their formal harassment or grievance procedures. Or – if you feel that your employer is the bully – from outside support such as a trade union. You cannot make a legal claim directly about bullying, but complaints can be made under laws covering discrimination and harassment. If you are forced to resign due to bullying you may be able to make a claim for constructive dismissal.

Even if you are sure that you have "just cause" to fight back against bullying, don't forget to take into account the overall situation you're in. There are times when it is best to leave an employer if you're being bullied and nothing is being done about it. I know someone who stayed in a position where he was bullied for years because he felt "It's not fair! I don't see why I should be forced out!" Fair or not, his health deteriorated and only improved when he finally decided to leave for another job.

- *If you are in the UK, you can find out more about dealing with bullying in the workplace here:* www.gov.uk/workplace-bullying-and-harassment

- *If you are in the US, you can find out more about dealing with bullying in the workplace through the Workplace Bullying Institute:* www.workplacebullying.org

- *For help in dealing with workplace grievance and disciplinary issues, check out this useful guide from the Department for Education, Business and Skills:* http://bis.ecgroup.net/Publications/EmploymentMatters/ResolvingDisputes/091226.aspx

Keep away from people who try to belittle your ambitions. Small people always do that, but the really great make you feel that you, too, can become great.

~ Mark Twain

CHAPTER 12
GETTING AN EMPLOYER'S ATTENTION

No employer today is independent of those about him.
He cannot succeed alone, no matter how great his
ability or capital. Business today is more than ever a
question of cooperation.

~ Orison Swett Marden

Approaching Employers

Now that you've identified your Vital Vocation (or some workable approximation of it), you're ready to strike out towards it. That could mean landing a job (or jobs) that you select and apply for, or creating one (or more) from scratch.

If you feel your vocation lies in self-employment, there are some strategies to get you started in Chapter 14, but in *this* chapter and the next, we're looking at how to apply for pre-existing jobs.

Although there are several avenues which can lead to a job, there are just two basic types of route:

- **One is finding a job through the traditional method of filling in an application form or sending a prospective employer your CV.**

- **The other is the less traditional (but often far more effective) method of making a more direct, personal approach to the employer.**

We'll look at each one in turn, but first we'll look at how you can construct a compelling written "pitch" for a job – a great application form or curriculum vitae – then we'll find out how you can use a network of contacts to guide you to the employer with the right job for you (even one that hasn't been advertised).

Contacting Employers Effectively: CVs and Application Forms

According to Richard Nelson Bolles in his book *What Color is Your Parachute?*, sending CVs or application forms to employers can have a success rate ranging from just 7% (if you apply randomly) to 24% (if you target specific employers). These are not fantastic odds, but it's still worth using these techniques, particularly if you're applying for a job that you know you're qualified to do. Just remember that it would be unwise to pursue this as your *only* job-search method. Treat it as one part of your job-hunting arsenal and make sure you do it right.

So, how do you do it right?

If you Google "writing a CV" on the internet, you'll find lots of information on this topic. Here are some key points to remember when writing a CV or filling in an application form:

1. **Always follow instructions**. You'd be amazed at how many people don't. I've been involved in recruiting people into jobs for nearly 20 years and it never ceases to amaze me how many applicants will fall at this first hurdle because they fail to observe the word limit on an application form, or don't lay out the answers the way they were instructed to. Read *all* the instructions on an application form before beginning. Then read them again. Twice!

2. **Use a reliable template**. This applies to CVs. Find a model that you like and that is suitable for the industry you're applying to. In general, CVs should be no more than two sides of A4 paper and should contain some key components: your contact details; your employment history (most recent first); your key skills and talents (as demonstrated by your employment); relevant qualifications (you probably don't need

to list details of your primary school!); memberships; published work; and – if available – details of testimonials from colleagues and clients. Depending on available room, you may be able to include a general statement about your ambitions, but this will depend on your feelings about the employer you're sending it to.

3. **Tailor it.** You will almost never want to send the same CV to several employers, or to use exactly the same information on different application forms. You need to consider how the information you could share is relevant to the situation at hand. Carefully study the requirements of the job you're applying for and the person specification (if one is supplied) and use that as a prompt for the information you include.

4. **Draw out your achievements.** Employers use CVs and application forms to weed out applicants, whittling them down to a few that they can invite to interview. From your point of view, then, it's important that what you write catches their attention. That doesn't mean writing something that's "way out" in an effort to surprise them (unless you're applying to be a comedian).

   Richard Nelson Bolles recommends using the acronym "**EASY**" to help in drawing out your achievements. When discussing a previous (or current) job role, you want to make mention of your **Experiences** in the job, any relevant **Achievements** therein, the **Skills** you developed and **Your** understanding of how this links to the job you're applying for.

5. **Enclose a return envelope and note.** Your chances or receiving a reply from an employer – even if it's a rejection – will be greatly increased if you take the trouble to enclose a self-addressed envelope with your CV or application form, and a covering letter explaining that you're pleased to be applying for their job and look forward to hearing from them in due course. It's not a guarantee that they'll reply – indeed, some employers even specify that they *don't* reply to anyone except successful applicants – but it's polite and it will undoubtedly mark you out from the majority of applicants. Don't underestimate how powerful this demonstration of thoughtfulness can be.

Filling in a Job Application Effectively

Here's some simple step-by-step advice on job applications:

1. **Consider what the employer wants.** Every vacancy will require a unique set of qualities and competencies, but there are some transferable skills which employers look for again and again. Take time to find out about the job and make a note of the kinds of skills that the employer is likely to be looking for. Don't forget to consider how your own unique talents can apply to this job.

   Transferable skills can include: *initiative, willingness to learn, interpersonal skills, communication, teamwork, flexibility, motivation, numeracy, computer literacy, etc.* Give examples of the skills you possess, referring to previous jobs, to voluntary work, to your education and even to your home responsibilities (if you look after a household, you undoubtedly have budgetary and financial management experience). Use the Skills Checklist in Chapter 5 to prompt you.

2. **Construct your application carefully.** Summarise the relevant parts of your education (most recent is most important and you don't have to list every qualification if it isn't relevant). Summarise your employment and work experience (most recent first). Describe the responsibilities and achievements in your previous roles that relate directly to the skills required in the job you are applying for. You can group together some experiences if space is limited.

   Outline some of your extracurricular activities and relate them to the skills required. It is more important to demonstrate *relevant* skills and experiences than to list amazing achievements; don't try to impress the employer, just be honest and relevant. Provide references, one of which should be work-related if possible.

   To promote your relevant competencies, you must address all the points on the person specification in the order in which they appear; in fact, it's often a good idea to use them as headings. Imagine the specification is being used as a checklist by the person who's short-listing (it is).

Address each point on the job specification in a clearly headed paragraph. In your first sentence, summarise how you meet the specific requirement and then provide a recent example of how you have successfully demonstrated that specific attribute. Work experiences are especially convincing to employers. Remember to focus on how you successfully carried out the activity and the result you achieved, not just on what you did.

3. **Demonstrate that you understand the employer's ethos**. You may be asked to complete a personal statement which outlines your reasons for applying. You should describe what attracts you to the organisation and the specific role. Your statement should enthusiastically demonstrate a clear understanding of the organisation's motives, values and ethos and how they match your own, and also a sound appreciation of the role and why it suits your specific skills and talents.

Needless to say, the more research you do to identify attractive features of the job and organisation so that you can mention them knowledgably in the application, the better.

4. **Avoid common mistakes**. The most common mistakes that could prevent you from getting an interview include: poor spelling and grammar (check, check and check again), not answering the questions (make sure you understand the question being asked before beginning to answer it), not being clear about your results (don't just say *what* you did, give examples of *how* you did things and the good outcomes you achieved as a result), and underselling yourself (see point 1 above and remember to fully consider what the employer wants).

Writing a Great CV

There are many useful (and free) templates for CVs available online, along with tips on how to write them. Take a look and see what fits you best. In the meantime, here's a basic, good CV outline that can be adapted to almost any situation. Try to keep it to two sides of A4 paper only; it stands more of a chance of being read that way.

<u>**YOUR NAME & Qualifications, e.g. MA, PhD**</u>

Address, telephone number, email address – all on one line

Paragraph summarising who/what you are, what you offer and what you are seeking. Bold for this section, with a box around it. This can be the most difficult part and should normally be left to last. Keep it to no more than four lines of text.

- Key Skills bullet points
- No more than five or six
- Keep them to one line each
- Use "action words" (e.g. supervising)

CAREER & ACHIEVEMENTS

CURRENT/LAST EMPLOYER, location (Town and County) Jan 20xx – Present

Job Title – Brief description of role and responsibility, its context (size of department/company, etc.) and whom you reported to.

- List of achievements: what you actually made happen
- Bullet points: more detail can be given at an interview
- Probably no more than five points per job
- No more than two lines each
- Use them to highlight things that you want an interviewer to raise for discussion

PREVIOUS EMPLOYER #1, location (Town and County) Oct 20xx – Dec 20xx

Job Title – Brief description of role and responsibility, its context (size of department/company, etc.) and whom you reported to.

- xxxx
- xxxxx
- xxxxxx

PREVIOUS EMPLOYER #2, location (Town and County) Feb 20xx – Sept 20xx

Move this whole third employer to page 2 if necessary (do not split this section over two pages).

Job Title – Brief description of role and responsibility, its context (size of department/company, etc.) and whom you reported to. With some employers you will have been in more than one role, which should be shown like this.

- xxxxx
- xxxxxx
- xxxxxxx

Job Title – Brief description of role and responsibility, its context (size of department/company, etc.) and whom you reported to.

- xxxxx
- xxxxxx
- xxxxxxx

SUMMARY OF ANY PREVIOUS EMPLOYMENT   19xx – 20xx

- Simply list employers, roles and achievements in summary form
- More detail can be covered at the interview if the interviewer wishes
- xxxxxxxxxxxxx

EDUCATION, QUALIFICATIONS & PROFESSIONAL MEMBERSHIPS

A summary of what you have achieved) e.g.

- Chartered Engineer (CEng)
- Fellow of the Royal Society of Arts (FRSA)
- University: Degree, Subject xxxxxxxxxx   19xx – 19xx
- School: Highest qualifications followed by lower qualifications if needed   19xx – 19xx

FURTHER PROFESSIONAL ACTIVITY

Optional section where you can include, in summary form:

- Training courses attended
- Professional activities, such as speaking at conferences, involvement with learned bodies and/or trade associations
- Continuous professional development activities undertaken

PERSONAL

Here you can give what details you wish, but keep it short:

- Date of birth: 12/12/19xx
- Status: Married, X children
- Nationality: xxxxxxxxxxx
- Driving licence: xxx
- Hobbies/Leisure activities and interests (include clubs, sports, interests, charity work, etc. but keep short and to the point)

Don't wait until you've found a specific job to apply for before refreshing your CV. If you do it now, you'll be able to use it when a job does appear and you can also use the material in the CV for application forms if you're required to fill out any of those.

EXERCISE 23: Preparing Your CV

Set aside an hour or two and draft an outline for a new (or refreshed) CV using the template above. Include the relevant information as suggested in the template and make a note of any other information you may wish to use to tailor the CV to specific jobs. You can use this material for application forms, too.

Getting an Employer's Attention: The Importance of the Direct Approach

Many of us have got used to thinking that a job application or CV is a necessary step towards getting through an employer's door for an interview and ultimately for a job. However, if you can find the right way of connecting *personally* with a prospective employer, then you may be able to make great progress before you even have to deploy your CV.

The right way of connecting will vary from employer to employer, but there are two important components that need to be in place in order to maximise your chances of success:

1. **You need to find employers who *aren't* currently advertising their vacancies, as well as those who *are*.**

2. **You need to identify the person with the power to hire and fire in either type of organisation.**

By considering organisations who aren't currently advertising vacancies, you're taking full advantage of the fact that many jobs are never advertised (estimates suggest that perhaps *most* available jobs - as many of 65% - are never formally advertised).

Many job-hunters will wait until an employer *invites* applications.

You're not going to wait for an invitation. If an employer looks like it meets your Vital Vocation criteria, and as though it *might* have jobs that fit the bill for you, you're going to make contact straight away. That way, you'll massively increase your chances of accessing that 65% of unadvertised jobs.

I have one client who has found not one but *two* part-time jobs, with different employers, by approaching them directly when they weren't advertising any vacancies. He was able to indicate to them how his skills with computers could be put to good use for them. As a result, he has two jobs that he enjoys and which still leave him enough spare time to pursue his real passion, which is gardening.

Once you've identified the organisations that interest you, you then need to do some investigating to find out who has the hire/fire power, and then you need to network your way to them.

Sounds complicated, doesn't it? In fact, it's relatively simple, but it takes practice and persistence (you may not find your first attempt is successful, but don't let that put you off).

Since at least some of the organisations you target are likely to be quite small (i.e. those that are not advertising their vacancies), you're almost certainly going to find it much easier to connect with those than with the larger employers out there.

Here's a step-by-step process to follow when you're ready to make the direct approach:

 How To Make the Direct Approach

Step 1: Identify your prospective employers.

Make a list of all the employers who are "prospects" – in other words, those who could hire you to carry out your Vital Vocation. Use your own memory first then check the internet and phone book. Ask your contacts too (more on that in a moment). Make sure the employers you select fit the criteria of your Vital Vocation in terms of the four factors outlined in Chapter 1.

Step 2: Ask your existing contacts to help you find a way in.

This could be as simple as giving you the name of the HR manager, whom you could then call or write to. Or they may even know someone who knows someone who could get you an appointment.

Contact as many people as you can – family members, friends, friends of friends, current colleagues, ex-colleagues, fellow members of any institutions you belong to, people who you're in contact with on social media sites, members of your Vital Vocation Dream Team (see Chapter 11) – and ask them if they know anyone who works at your prospective employer. If they do, put them to work finding out whom you need to speak to and – if you feel it's appropriate – making it known that you are interested in working there.

You'd be surprised at how well this works. I got two of my best jobs as a student through networking in just this manner. You may only at this stage be able to get the contact details of someone who works at the prospective employer, but who isn't the hirer and firer. That's fine, because it's one step closer. You'll still want to speak to them and once you've built a rapport, you could ask *them* to introduce you to the person you need to see.

Step 3: Make an appointment.

As soon as you know who has the power to hire you, you need to speak to them. You could do this by calling up and making an appointment directly. But if you've only got the contact details of someone who works there but doesn't have the power to hire or fire, make an appointment with them instead and use it to find out more about the place. Keep doing this until you are able to make direct contact with the hirer/firer.

Step 4: Describe what you have to offer.

Once you've got some time with the hirer/firer, you need to demonstrate to them that you have something – in fact, a lot! – to offer their organisation. Don't do this by browbeating them; do it by having a discussion with them. In making the appointment, make it clear you'll take no more than 25 minutes of their time (less if that's all they have) and use that time to engage with them about the subject area the employer (and your Vital Vocation) relates to.

This is the very way that several of my clients have got hired for an ideal job – because the connection between them and the employer was obvious. The chances of this happening in normal circumstances are, of course, remote; but when you're going after your Vital Vocation, you'll find the chances multiply exponentially, since you'll be already approaching employers who are a good "fit" for you.

You should, of course, leave some information behind. Not a voluminous folder of photocopies of every qualification or award you've ever accumulated: a copy of your (tailored) CV will be sufficient.

Important: *Always make it easy for the employer to communicate with you.* Be prepared to make follow-up calls or to send a note to your contact after a phone call has been made. If you write, enclose a self-addressed envelope so they can easily write back.

Don't resent doing this, even if you feel the employer has enough resources to cover the cost of postage. That isn't the point. You want them to see you as someone who is prepared to make an effort. For that same reason, *always* – even if your efforts go unrewarded at first – write to thank them for their time and consideration.

Remember: estimates suggest that, at any given time, upwards of 65% of available jobs are not advertised to the marketplace and are therefore *only likely to be filled through word-of-mouth and direct contacts*. That's why you should seriously consider this approach. It'll bring *you* into contact with opportunities that won't be visible to you otherwise, or to most of the job-hunting population.

Social Media: Getting an Employer's Attention the *Right* Way

There is no doubt that social media platforms are key players in the job-hunt and career-change process today. Sites like LinkedIn, Facebook, Google+, and Meetup are great ways of connecting positively with other job-hunters, career-changers or new business-builders.

Social media can also be a great way of identifying the "hirers and firers" you need to contact within a workplace in order to make the direct approach outlined above. It's becoming increasingly easy to find out who does what in an organisation through their web or social media presence. Some companies have Facebook pages or LinkedIn profiles which are publicly viewable, and which can offer real insights into what their working environment and organisational culture is really like. Asking a polite question in one of these groups can be a great way of getting some useful information "straight from the horse's mouth".

Josh Tolan, CEO of SparkHire, points out in a post on the Mashable blog (http://mashable.com/2012/12/16/crowdsource-your-job-hunt/) that it's possible to use social media to "crowdsource" inquiries into such areas as decision-makers, corporate culture, and even likely interview questions. He says:

> *"If you're not directly linked with anyone in your company of choice, you can always ask a connection to help you reach out. Utilize big social media networks like Facebook and Twitter to find current and former employees, then ask if they have a few moments to talk about the company. Most professionals are eager to help others and make new contacts and will be thrilled you turned to them as thought leaders."*

A note of caution, however. Be aware that recent estimates suggest that as many as 37% of employers use social media sites to "screen" candidates, and of those who do, 65% say they do it to see if the job seeker presents himself or herself professionally (CareerBuilder survey, 2012: http://www.forbes.com/sites/jacquelynsmith/2013/04/16/how-social-media-can-help-or-hurt-your-job-search/).

By all means, use social media to network, to present your wares - your own website or social media profile can work as an extended business card or CV - and to investigate the field of your Vital Vocation. Just make sure that the "you" you present online is one that makes a positive impression. If you wouldn't be happy for someone to see you a particular way in "real life", you shouldn't want them to see you that way online.

All is not doom and gloom. The CareerBuilder survey mentioned above also indicated that 29% of hiring employers using this method found something positive on a social media profile that prompted them to offer the candidate a job.

Brad Schepp, author of How *To Find A Job On LinkedIn, Facebook, Twitter and Google+*, has some useful advice to offer:

> *"Make sure any profiles you write are free of typos, the information is coherent and applicable to your industry (or job you're trying to land), and your photos present you in a favorable light. You can verify the applicability of the information by checking profiles of others in the same field. Don't assume an employer will only be checking you out on LinkedIn. They may also check Facebook, or even Twitter and*

Google+. The story you tell on each site should be pretty much the same, although it's fine to adapt the material for the site."

Remember: Contacts are the Key

I'm going to finish with an illustrative story that Richard Nelson Bolles tells about the process I've outlined here, and the importance of the direct approach. In his classic job-hunting and career-changing manual, *What Color is Your Parachute?*, he says:

> *"My favourite (true) story in this regard concerns a job-hunter I know... He decided he wanted to work for a particular health-care organisation... Not knowing any better, he approached them (by) filling in an application form ... he was told there were no jobs available. Stop. Period. End of story.*
>
> *"Approximately three months later he learned about this technique of approaching your favourite organisation by using contacts. He explored his contacts diligently and succeeded in getting an interview with the person-who-had-the-power-to-hire-him for the position he was interested in. The two of them hit it off, immediately. The appointment went swimmingly. 'You're hired,' said the person-who-had-the-power-to-hire-him. 'I'll call Human Resources and tell them you're hired, and that you'll be down to fill out the necessary stuff.'*
>
> *"Our job-hunter never once mentioned that he had previously approached that same organisation through that same Human Resources Department and had been turned down cold.*
>
> *"Just remember: contacts are the key. It takes about eighty pairs of eyes and ears to help find the career, the workplace, the job that you are looking for. Your contacts are those eighty eyes and ears."*

(Bolles, 2010, p. 66)

CHAPTER 13
HOW TO ACE THE INTERVIEW

At interviews, be yourself – but the best half of yourself.

~ John Courtis

Attending a job interview is one of the most nerve-wracking parts of the job-hunt or career-change process. When the job in question is your dream job, the stakes are even higher and the pressure can feel higher still.

This chapter will break the interview process down for you in a way that makes it manageable and easier to prepare for. In approaching any interview, you need to consider two key areas of focus:

1. **The way you present yourself in the broadest sense to the employing company.**

2. **The way you present yourself in a specific sense, on the day of the interview, to the people who are conducting the interview. This includes the practical approach you take to the interview itself and any associated tests.**

One step at a time, this chapter will help you to ace your interviews.

What is an Interview?

The common view of the job interview is that it's a conversation for an employer's benefit, designed to help them establish if they want to hire you (the interviewee) for a particular job. From the interviewee's perspective however, it's something more important than that. It's about making positive connections with a prospective employer. It's an opportunity for you to demonstrate that you are the solution to their problems. It's a chance for you to display (and sometimes even discover) your best self. And - importantly - it's also a chance for you to suss *them* out. In a sense, you're interviewing the employing organisation as much as they're interviewing you.

Getting Ready to Present Yourself

It's quite common to think of an interview as a chance to "sell" yourself to the prospective employer. However, this can lead to an approach which is far pushier than it needs to be. The fact is, if you're being interviewed, the employer has already decided that you're potentially employable. Your job, during the interview, is to communicate with the interviewer in a way that allows both of you to make a couple of key decisions.

- **You** need to decide if you want to work there, in that job, for that employer – or not.

- The **employer** needs to decide that you, of all the people they're seeing, are right for the job – or not.

The first step of preparing for an interview is to consider the "you" that you're going to present to the employer.

A key thing to bear in mind is that the interviewer will be feeling nervous too. They're faced with an important task – to fill a vacancy. If doing so wasn't important to them, they wouldn't be doing it. Consequently, you want to present yourself as *the best possible solution to the employer's pressing problem or need.*

You can carry out the next exercise when you're preparing for an interview. Better yet, go through the exercise *before* you have any interviews lined up. It won't do you any harm to be prepared well in advance!

EXERCISE 24: Interview Preparation

Step 1: Consider how you'll look when they first encounter you.

Do some research on the dress code of the place you're applying to. There isn't a hard-and-fast rule here, despite what some recruitment consultants might tell you. Although you might want to dress a bit more conservatively than you would on the job, you still want to reflect the culture and dress code of the employer. That's going to be different, depending on whether you're applying for a job at a bank, or a circus! You'll also want to be comfortable. If it's a hot day, you may want to wear lighter materials, for example. And, it goes without saying, make sure that - whatever clothes you're wearing - both you and they are clean and presentable.

Step 2: Consider how you'll appear to them as they see you in action.

Nervous mannerisms, speaking too quietly, speaking too loudly, laughing inappropriately, being too flippant, being too serious, constantly interrupting the interviewer, giving monosyllabic answers to questions, false modesty, unbridled arrogance – these are all likely to put employers off. You need to strike the right balance and the best way to do that is to enter the process feeling as calm as possible. You will be experiencing some stress – that's natural – but take some time beforehand to compose yourself by taking a few deep breaths. Remind yourself of the stress-busting techniques from Chapter 8 if you need to. And use them!

Step 3: Consider your behaviour both before and after the interview.

Even in this age of equal opportunity and tight recruitment processes, don't for a minute think that you're only being judged on how you perform in the actual interview. If you are rude to the receptionist when you arrive, discourteous to other interview candidates, or unwilling to engage with the interviewer after the interview has finished, you will be disadvantaging yourself. Remind yourself that you are "on" as soon as you arrive for the interview and you're not "off" again until you're safely home afterwards!

Step 4: Prepare your attitude.

You can directly influence the atmosphere of an interview by your own attitude to it. Decide up-front that you are going to expect a warm welcome, a friendly discussion, positive feedback and a positive outcome (whether or not you get the job) rather than a cold reception, hostile questions, conflict, criticism and a negative outcome – and act accordingly.

 Self-Coaching Questions

1. What changes can you make to your wardrobe now in order to make things easier for you at your next interview?

2. What are likely to be the aspects of the interview you'll find most nerve-wracking? What techniques will you use to help yourself through stressful moments? Check back to Chapter 8 for some ideas.

3. What are the key positive characteristics you want to demonstrate to a prospective employer? How will you embody them at an interview?

Now, let's look more closely at the two key areas of focus when dealing with an interview:

Interview Key Focus Area 1: Approaching the Company

It's very important to develop an understanding of your prospective employer before the interview. The reasons for this are as follows:

- By understanding the company you are aiming to be hired by, you'll be able to demonstrate this at an interview, which is likely to impress the interviewer.

- By understanding the psychology of the interviewer, you'll be able to make it easier for them to recognise you as the right person for the job.

- The more you learn about the company before the interview, the more you're likely to understand the questions you're asked on the day.

Here are the key elements to remember:

1. **Do your research**. Visit their website, speak to people who know about the company, read their business plan if they have one, search the internet for news stories about them, download any brochures they have online. In short, do the homework you need to do in order to enter the interview fully armed with knowledge about the company.

   This really will set you above the crowd because – sad to say – this is precisely what most applicants don't do. If you're one of the few who do, the interviewer's confidence that you're seriously interested will rise significantly. You'll also be able to ask intelligent questions when the opportunity arises, instead of stock questions which are likely to bore the interviewer to tears.

2. **Appreciate that the interviewer has a goal**. Many people enter interviews as though they're expecting an experience that has been intentionally designed to be an ordeal. Bear in mind that the interviewer will be experiencing stress too; they will be actively looking for that moment of relief when they can feel

"I've done it! I've found the person to fill this vacancy!" Your goal is to get out of your own way, so that they can see that that person is *you*. Try to approach the interview with an air of shared cooperation; you're there to help the interviewer. You do that by being part of the solution to the company's problems.

3. **Be part of the solution**. Bear in mind the basics of what any employer will be looking for: punctuality, an ability to work hard, dependability, a focus on solutions rather than problems, a good attitude, energy, enthusiasm, self-discipline, motivation, etc. Use the research you do beforehand to discover any specific problems this employer is dealing with and demonstrate how you can provide solutions. For example, your research may indicate that the employer needs more staff that are able to work flexible hours. If you are, then you need to let them know this.

 ## Self-Coaching Questions

1. Based on what you already know about your Vital Vocation, what are the key characteristics of the employers most likely to hire you to do this type of job?

2. How will you go about reassuring an interviewer that you are the right person for the job? What preparation can you do before the interview to make your positive approach even more likely?

3. How will you ensure you find out about the specific problems a prospective employer is dealing with? What can you do now to make such information more accessible to you?

Interview Key Focus Area 2: Approaching the Interview Itself

The moment is here. You're about to head into the interview. You've prepared – you're dressed appropriately, you've reminded yourself to be warm, polite and professional. You've done your research. So how do you handle the actual interview?

There's no magic wand that can make this most unnatural and unnerving of experiences easier, but if you go in with a strategy, you'll feel all the more confident. Here it is. If you can, read this before you leave the house for the interview or take it with you and read it while you're waiting to be seen.

The Interview Strategy

1. **Remember: the interviewer *wants* to hire you.** The interviewer is likely to be actively looking to fill a vacancy. Even if they are not, it is likely they won't want to miss out on the opportunity to hire someone who could add something positive to their company. Keep bearing this in mind. Rather than seeing them as a guard dog ferociously trying to keep you off their territory, see them as a kind guide trying to help both of you decide if this is a good "match".

2. **Keep your answers relevant and content-rich.** One of the purposes of the interview is for the interviewer to learn more about you; so, obviously, you're going to have to say quite a bit about yourself. To avoid rambling, talk about yourself only if what you say offers some benefit to the organisation. In answering questions, give evidence. For example, if they ask you how you handle yourself in a crisis, give an example of when you've handled a crisis well, along with details of what you did and the positive results you got.

3. **Observe the timings of your answers carefully.** If you have set up the interview in line with the instructions in Chapter 12, stick to your word of taking up no more than 25 minutes of their time (unless they specifically ask for more). Keep your answers brief, but comprehensive, and your questions to the point. Don't waffle. If you've been invited to an interview, you still need to be conscious of timing.

   In your answers to a question, try not to talk for longer than two minutes at a time. If you need to say more, pause and ask the interviewer if you're giving them the information they need. A failure to do this could lead you down a blind alley and not all interviewers will stop you.

4. **Ask questions and listen almost as much as you speak.** Research has shown that the people who are most likely to get hired after an interview are those who listen almost as much as they speak. This indicates that they have engaged fully in communication with the interviewer(s) and have asked some pertinent questions. By asking questions, you indicate you are genuinely interested. Questions can be asked during the interview (for clarity, but don't overdo the questions at this stage) and at the end (make sure you've prepared some questions beforehand – see below).

5. **Don't beg.** If you approach the interview on the basis that you have a valuable resource to offer the company, rather than by giving the impression you're desperate for work, you are likely to fare better. Take it as read that they know that you really, really want the job. You don't have to show that in the interview, but you do have to show that they should really, really want you to *do* the job. You do that by – again and again – demonstrating that you bring solutions to their problems.

6. **Leave them with evidence.** Unless the company interviewing you expressly forbids it, or unless you've already provided them with it, the end of the interview is a good time to present them with your CV and with any evidence of your work. In the case of a portfolio of work, bear in mind that they may not read it, so it would be worth drawing their attention to just one item that will be of particular interest to them.

Nine Questions You <u>Must</u> be Able to Answer

You may be worrying about some of the tough questions you'll be asked. A search on the internet will furnish you with examples of the kind of answers to give to a whole host of tough interview questions. What I've done here is to distil them into a few questions which you *must* be able to answer. Figure out your answers to these, and you'll find that almost every other question fits under the category of one of them.

1. **"Why have you applied for this job?"** This is all about the interviewer finding out why you've approached them rather than another company. Here's a great place for you to speak

about your Vital Vocation. Be enthusiastic, but avoid being effusive. You should also demonstrate your understanding of their company here, and your conviction that you are able to be a major contributor towards achieving their aims.

2. **"What are you offering us?"** This is where you can demonstrate how you can solve their problems. In answering this question (or others of its type) you will want to indicate how your experience, skills and talents are going to help the employer to run their business more effectively.

3. **"Tell us about yourself."** This is a very open question, which is inviting you to say something about yourself. What they really mean here is what kind of person are you? Will you fit in here? What will you add? How does your profile match our needs? They do not want to hear your entire life history or what you had for breakfast; they want information that's relevant to the position you're applying for.

4. **"Why should we choose you?"** In other words, what distinguishes you from their other applicants? It's here that you're going to have to convey that you have better work habits than others: that you work harder, faster and more thoroughly than others. You can't do a direct comparison with other candidates, of course, but you can illustrate your above-average performance level by reference to previous successes. Don't boast without backing yourself up; but, equally, don't be afraid to indicate why you really are the best candidate for the job.

5. **"Will you take the job if we offer it?"** You'd be surprised how many interviewers have this question in the back of their mind. It's not uncommon for a candidate to turn a job down after they've been offered it. Sometimes for good reason – such as a better offer – and sometimes for reasons that are intensely annoying to employers (e.g. "I didn't really want the job; I was just practising my interview skills for a more important interview.") They want reassurance that they're not wasting their time in seeing you. Give them that reassurance. If you can't, you shouldn't be in the interview in the first place.

6. **"What are your future career plans?"** Be prepared to talk

about your career plans and what you hope to achieve in the future. Most employers will find this attractive, but be careful not to give the impression that you're going to just use this job as a stepping stone, with a view to getting out of it as soon as possible. Even if that's the case, you'll want to reassure them that you're in it for the duration.

7. **"Why did you leave your last job?"** You're likely to be probed on this, especially if there are gaps in your employment history. Rehearse short, simple, positive answers to cover these points. Don't lie, but don't be afraid to put a positive "spin" on things if necessary. Most of all, be prepared for the question.

8. **"How will you handle a crisis?"** Most interviews will include a question in which you'll be given a difficult scenario and asked how you'd handle it (or how you've handled something similar in the past). I always ask this question when I'm interviewing people for jobs. I never cease to be dismayed by the number of people who clearly haven't anticipated that they might be asked something like this. Don't be one of them; come prepared with good examples.

9. **"What are your weaknesses?"** It's a clichéd question, but it usually comes up. The trick here is to shift emphasis onto your strengths as soon as possible. Avoid focusing on your personality flaws and talk about something you're in the process of changing, which may have a positive spin-off, such as, "I take too much time to switch out of work mode sometimes. I'm getting better at that transition [say how] and I do find that sometimes I'll think up solutions to a work issue when I'm out of work. I've learned to keep it in balance, so that I manage my energy."

Four Questions You <u>Should</u> Be Ready to Ask Them

You'll almost always be invited to ask an interviewer some questions. If they don't invite you, politely ask if you could just clarify one or two things and ask them anyway. Don't take too long to do this, but make your questioning genuine. Remember, you want to give them the clear impression that you're genuinely interested.

1. **"What else does the job involve?"** This is about reading between the lines of the job description (if there is one) and finding out as much as you can about what the job will actually entail. This is important; you need to have enough information to help you decide if the job is one that will meet the requirements of your Vital Vocation. Be enthusiastic in asking this question, but don't be afraid to use what you learn to think carefully about the answer you'll give if you're offered the job.

2. **"What are the company's plans for progress?"** This will help demonstrate your interest, but will also furnish you with a good idea of where things are going in this prospective workplace. Based on their answer, you can work out what a period of time working here could do for your career plans.

3. **"How will you help me to develop my skills?"** This indicates a keenness on your part to develop and grow (a characteristic that should be attractive to an employer) and also gives you a chance to suss out what kinds of support systems they have in place. What form of appraisal do they use? What reporting and monitoring mechanisms do they have? What training and personal development opportunities are there?

4. **"What happens next?"** You want to leave with a clear indication of when you'll hear back from them, so if they don't automatically tell you – ask!

One final thing you may want to ask about is the salary you'll be paid. This is an important part of the negotiation and you shouldn't shy away from it. If they can't offer you the job at a salary that will genuinely keep you (and remember, it may not be your ideal salary at first) then you need to know this as soon as possible.

As a general rule of thumb, however, you should not attempt to negotiate your salary upwards until you've been offered the job. If you try to do this too early, you run the risk of giving the impression that the salary is your main interest and that may not play in your favour. Some good variations of this question might be:

- *"How much are you offering as a salary for this post?"*

- *"Are there any other benefits? Is the salary negotiable?"*

- *"Would you consider starting me midway through the salary scale?"*

Congratulations! With the information you've just covered, you've rocketed yourself into the minority of people who are fully equipped to handle a job interview with a sure hand.

Good luck!

Death will be a great relief. No more interviews.

~ Katharine Hepburn

CHAPTER 14
FLYING SOLO: ARE YOU AN
ENTREPRENEUR?

Be nice to geeks.
You'll probably end up working for one.

~ Bill Gates

Sometimes, your Vital Vocation doesn't actually exist until you create it. In this chapter - which is an offering to those of you who've come to see that your Vital Vocation is to set up your *own* business rather than working for someone else's - we're going to look briefly at:

- **How to go about setting up your own business**

- **Working freelance**

- **Creating your own non-profit social enterprise**

It's beyond the scope of this book to go into these topics in detail, so consider the sections that follow as "jumping-off" points. Each one will take you through the basic considerations and give you suggestions of where to go for further information and support.

Whichever of the above options is of particular interest to you, you'll find the business plan template I've provided in this chapter really useful.

Building Your Own Business: Self-Test

Building a business isn't for everyone. If it's for you, you'll already have recognised that you have certain characteristics. How many of the following can you tick?

- ☐ **You commonly have enterprising ideas**

- ☐ **You're perceptive to the needs of your community, world, potential market**

- ☐ **You're creative in conceiving ways to provide for that need**

- ☐ **You can identify ways to finance your idea**

- ☐ **You feel comfortable with the notion of taking responsibility for generating income to further your idea**

- ☐ **You're courageous and willing to try something new, even if it's a step in the dark**

- ☐ **You have initiative and are able to work incredibly hard, even when you're exhausted**

- ☐ **You have the determination to stick with it, even in the midst of setbacks and frustrations – and even when everyone is telling you it can't be done.**

If you don't recognise several of these qualities in yourself, then be kind to yourself and don't attempt to set up a business on your own.

What's Your Niche?

Any successful business operates within a "niche" of some sort. In other words, it delivers a particular kind of product or service to a particular customer base. You need to determine what your product/service will be and who you're going to market it to.

Barbara Winter, in her excellent book *Making a Living Without a Job*, outlines the best method for finding a niche I've ever come across.

She says:

"In identifying your niche, keep in mind that it will be a group with whom you share a bond. Your niche is a group that you are already part of or know a great deal about because you share its problems or interests. A niche isn't 'them' – it's 'us'. Stay focused on serving the market you know well. Once you have developed one market niche, you may find it's a simple matter to identify another and repeat the process." (Making a Living Without a Job, 2009 edition, p. 205)

So, what's your niche? Who around you needs help? What kind of help do they need? How can you provide for at least part of that need? Determining the answers to such questions can be the most important first step in building a successful business.

EXERCISE 25: Step-by-Step to a Brand New Business

Follow this step-by-step process to generate business ideas and a plan for developing them.

Step 1: Draw the Outline of Your Potential Business

- What need do you see around you that you'd like to address?
- What solution to that need do you think is required?
- Which of your own talents can help provide that solution?
- What product/service could provide that solution?
- Where could you get ideas for potential products/services?
- What similar products/services are meeting similar needs? What can you learn from them?

- What product/service are you able to offer, based on your unique skills and abilities?
- How will your product/service be used?
- What unique features can you bring to its design, delivery and marketing?
- Who is your major competition?
- What are their strengths and weaknesses?
- How will you distinguish yourself from the competition?
- How will you deliver your product/service?

Step 2: Research Your Market

- Remember, your niche is not "them", it's "us". Who are your community? Is it a small group (e.g. "single parents in my town") or wider (e.g. "women")?
- Within that community, identify the potential buyers of your product/service by considering their characteristics: age, sex, ethnicity, class, purchasing power, profession, cultural characteristics.
- Where is your prospective market based? In which country, region, city, neighbourhood, environment?
- What is their lifestyle? What activities do they pursue? What do they do in their spare time?
- Where do they hang out?
- Using the variables above, can you write a sketch of your potential market?

Step 3: Decide How to Communicate

- How will you get the attention of your market? By word of mouth, leaflets, adverts in the press, promotional appearances and speeches, magazines, television, radio, introductory seminars, writing books and publications, the internet, blogs, newsletters, direct mail, telephone canvassing, other?

- How will you distribute your product/service? By retail, mail order, online, franchising, telemarketing, other?

Step 4: Build Support

- What skills will you need to ask others to provide to help get your business started?

- Who will handle the management of the process? The accountancy? The advertising? The legal aspects? The marketing strategy? The selling?

- What other support functions might you need?

- What undeveloped skills can you compensate for by having an individual on your team who has that strength?

Step 5: Balance the Books

- Consider the costs of your prospective business: equipment, furnishing, staff, start-up inventory, premises costs, professional services, advertising, office costs, start-up cash, and other miscellaneous costs.

- Work out your monthly operating costs: rent, utilities, postage, wages, taxes, printing, inventory, other.

- Decide how you'll raise money (if you need to). By a loan, credit union, investment consultant, suppliers giving credit, savings?

- Look on Amazon for suggestions of books on how to raise finance for a new business.

Step 6: Make It Legal

- What do you need to find out about the best legal structure to adopt?

- Will you work as a sole trader? A partnership? A limited company?

- Who can you contact for advice on such matters?

Step 7: Write A Business Plan

- What sort of business plan will you need? A very detailed one (if you're setting up a substantial business) or something quite simple (if you're a sole trader offering a service)?

Business Planning

Start-up businesses don't necessarily need detailed business plans at first. In fact, many businesses start and grow without them, but if you're thinking of borrowing money or asking others to "buy in" to your plans, it's not a bad idea to have a basic business plan in place. It can also help you to get your thoughts straight and your business ambitions down on paper.

There are several good template business plans available online, but to get you started, here's a basic outline. If you're going to write a business plan, it should at *least* cover these areas. If the most you can write now is a paragraph under each heading, that's fine; it's better than nothing and can be expanded later.

Basic Business Plan

Introduction

Executive summary: an overview of the plan and its contents.

Vision

The business idea: a brief description of your business concept.

Business goals: two or three things your concept is aiming to achieve.

What the business does: what is the practical activity of the business?

Marketing

Market research: why do you know this business is needed – what evidence do you have?

Profiling customers: details of the kind of people who'll use the business.

Promotion and advertising: how you will ensure potential customers know about it.

Running the business

Staff, premises and equipment: any practical considerations.

Finances

Start-up costs: what are they?

Profit and loss forecast: a basic estimated budget, ideally for the first six months.

Sourcing finance: where you will get any start-up resources from.

Managing financial risks: what contingency plans are in place if you can't get the money you need?

Are You a Social Entrepreneur?

How wonderful it is that nobody need wait a single moment before starting to improve the world.

~ Anne Frank

Do you want to change the world? If you want your business to have a specific, positive impact on society, beyond its bottom-line financial profits, you could be a "social entrepreneur".

Social entrepreneurs use a business model to address a social need. They set up "social ventures", also known as "social enterprises".

A social venture is basically a business, but with an additional bottom line beyond making a profit: making a difference or solving a social problem. Not-for-profit charitable organisations sometimes have "trading arms", which are social ventures that help support the non-profit's charitable objectives. Think of the store at the art gallery, or the community centre cafeteria that specifically employs and trains staff with disabilities. The charity I lead has its own trading arm which generates income for the charity through offering managed conferencing space for other charities and public bodies.

Social entrepreneurship has become very popular in recent years on both sides of the Atlantic, with a number of universities hosting social entrepreneur business competitions and establishing courses of study in how to set up businesses that do good while making a profit. Governments, too, are active in encouraging people to set up social enterprises, recognising that they can have an economic as well as a social benefit.

As chief executive of The Centre for Voluntary Action, (www.bvsc.org), a great deal of my work revolves around supporting social entrepreneurs and I'm a great believer in this business model, provided it's the right business model for the person or group concerned. It's important to realise that social entrepreneurship isn't a "softer" option for someone with a desire to set up a business. In fact, it's subject to many of the same difficulties and pressures that all businesses face and a few more besides.

So, why should you do it? For the same reason you should set up any business, or pursue any vocation: if it's the best possible way for you to express the fullness of who you are, including your talents, your skills, you values and your environmental preferences.

If you see a need in the world and believe that it can best be met by setting up a social enterprise then by all means go for it.

The Ten Key Characteristics of Social Entrepreneurs

In their 2008 book, *Power of Unreasonable People: How Social Entrepreneurs Create Markets that Change the World*, John Elkington and Pamela Hartigan set out the ten characteristics which their research indicated were prevalent amongst social entrepreneurs. Do you recognise yourself in these? If so, you could be social entrepreneur.

> *"Social entrepreneurs:*
> - *Try to shrug off the constraints of ideology or discipline;*
> - *Identify and apply practical solutions to social problems, combining innovation, resourcefulness and opportunity;*

- *Innovate by finding a new product, service or approach to a social problem;*
- *Focus first and foremost on social value creation and, in that spirit, are willing to share their innovations and insights for others to replicate;*
- *Jump in before ensuring that they are fully resourced;*
- *Have an unwavering belief in everyone's innate capacity, often regardless of education, to contribute meaningfully to economic and social development;*
- *Show a dogged determination that pushes them to take risks that others wouldn't dare;*
- *Balance their passion for change with the zeal to measure and monitor impact;*
- *Have a great deal to teach change-makers in other sectors;*
- *Display a healthy impatience."*

(Elkington and Hartigan, 2008, p. 5)

If these characteristics resonate with you, you can use the self-coaching questions you used in the previous section to help you determine the form that your social enterprise might take.

How to Set Up a Social Enterprise

If you are interested in setting up a UK-based social enterprise, I recommend you check out this Business Link Guide to Social Enterprises: https://www.gov.uk/set-up-a-social-enterprise

If you are interested in setting up a US-based social enterprise, see this Management Help Guide to Starting a Social Enterprise: http://managementhelp.org/startingorganizations/start-nonprofit.htm

The great use of life is in spending it for something that will outlast it.

~ William James

CHAPTER 15
LIFE ON THE OTHER SIDE:
HOW TO BE THE CEO OF YOU

You work that you may keep pace with the earth and the soul of the earth.
For to be idle is to become a stranger unto the seasons, and to step out of life's procession, that marches in majesty and proud submission towards the infinite. When you work you are a flute through whose heart the whispering of the hours turns to music.

~ Kahlil Gibran, *On Work*

Making a Positive Impact on Your First Day and Every Day

What a journey you've been on. From figuring out what you wanted to do with your life, you moved onto the practicalities of how to do it.

This chapter is about how to handle yourself once you've reached your goal and about making the most of where you are now whilst preparing yourself to meet the future head-on.

First, we're going to look at how you can make a positive impact in your new Vital Vocation in order to assure your future success. Then, we're going to examine how you can approach the job market of the future in order to ensure that your Vital Vocation remains at the heart of it.

Your First Day Onwards

Once you've found – or created – the job of your dreams, you can certainly congratulate yourself and take some time out to celebrate. Of course, your work isn't over. Now you have the task of holding onto that job, building it, refining it, developing yourself within it and ensuring that you make the most of the opportunity you've created for yourself. In short, you want to make a positive impact in the job on your first day and every day after that.

By making yourself as indispensable as you can (and there are limits to this, of course) you will create a level of security which can buffer you against the vagaries of an uncertain work environment and against the volatility of the future job market.

This doesn't mean that you won't have to look for work again in the future. You probably will, but isn't it great to know that you have the tools you've learned in this book to support you should a job hunt or career change become necessary?

To put you in the best place in your new job, I've put together a useful checklist.

The Six-Step Career Survival Plan

1. **Understand the work environment of today.** If you arm yourself with information about the way the working world works these days, you'll be creating an advantage for yourself that most people only dream of (see *The Career of the Future*, below). In addition to this "global picture", keep yourself abreast of developments in your field.

   No matter what position you hold in the organisation, you are the one who's responsible for your development and effectiveness. Take an interest in your employer's future plans, if you have any desire to be part of them, and take advantage of all the career development support that's available to you.

2. **Become an expert deliverer and influencer.** There are many different spheres of influence within any organisation. There's the broad "organisational structure", which includes everyone

who works there, and then there is a smaller network of key workers and influencers, made up of people at all levels who probably do most of the thinking and effective work within the organisation. No one will publicly declare who is in this group, but it's your job to discover it and make yourself a part of it.

Don't be a bystander – be a mover and shaker. Start small and slowly so you don't over-reach yourself, but work diligently to become part of this core group. It's by far the most secure group in the organisation and you'll find that – even when organisational structures change and jobs are lost – there will be a higher proportion of survivors in this group.

So, what are their characteristics and the characteristics you must embody? Delivery (in fact over-delivery) on promises; integrity in communications (no back-biting); support for others (pick up the slack when you need to, even if it's "not your job"). All of this will be noticed and will increase your influence and job security immeasurably.

3. **Make yourself indispensable**. Never stop growing and developing, and never rest on your laurels. Give more than is expected of you. Become an expert in your area of work. If you're doing what you most enjoy (and you should be if you've genuinely found your Vital Vocation), this won't be a problem. Keep up to date with advances in your field. Read about developments and speak to others, especially those at the cutting-edge of developments in the area.

4. **But don't make yourself obsolete!** There's no need to become paranoid about this or to let it hamper your ability to develop and train others when this is required (for example, when you're in a management position), but bear in mind that workplaces can be pretty competitive environments. Part of securing your position is about ensuring that others can't usurp it, either from within your peer group or from your direct reports.

The possibility of this occurring is greater when jobs are at risk. You never know when someone below or beside you in an organisation could be considered able to do your job, except more cheaply. It's unfair, but it does happen. So, whenever you are in a position of delegating or sharing authority, do it with tight reins and a clear indication of the essential contribution *you* make to the work. In other words, make sure that some essential facts and skills remain yours and yours alone, and make sure that the powers that be recognise that you are a valuable asset in that sense.

5. **Monitor and improve your own effectiveness.** You will probably be subject to monitoring and appraisal as part of your organisation's supervision structures, but no matter what else is in place, keep a close eye on your own delivery. The organisation's structures almost certainly won't keep track of all your genuine achievements, so it's *your* job to ensure they are acknowledged when appraisal time comes.

   If you're able to describe your successes, and back them up with examples, you'll be amazed at the effect this has on your career security and prospects. Unless your supervisors are threatened by your successes, they will almost certainly welcome them and want more. Most importantly, they will know that you are capable of giving them what they most need - solutions to their problems!

6. **Build in long-term goals, future alternatives and escape hatches!** Just because you've landed your dream job doesn't mean you should take your eye off a bigger-picture career plan. Whether or not you actively intend to leave your employer in the future, you need to prepare for the possibility that you will, whether you volunteer to do so or not. Keep clear in your mind what your long-range life and career goals are and you'll be better equipped to respond when circumstances change.

   Equally, you may be faced with opportunities in your current workplace and you want to be prepared to take advantage of them, rather than being confused by the options. Keep close inventory of your skills and don't be afraid to take some calculated risks to develop yourself when you get the chance.

   Finally, it never hurts to have some escape hatches, should you need to use them. Keeping the equivalent of three months of salary in the bank is a good discipline, in case you find yourself suddenly out of work. Also, consider building a "portfolio career" by developing your skills in an area of work that can earn you an income if the day job can't, for whatever reason.

The Career of the Future

Learn to love change. Master today's changes and tomorrow's uncertainties, because things are going to keep changing – with you or without you.

~ Bruce Tulgan, *Work This Way*

To ensure that you can have a life with your Vital Vocation at the heart of it, you need to be fully abreast of the latest thinking on the way the world of employment itself is developing. This awareness will mean that, whatever career you're pursuing, you can be aware of the skill-set, talents, values and environmental considerations that can support you in coping with a rapidly changing environment.

Some Predicted Future Work Trends

Here are some generally agreed trends that we are already seeing in the world of work and which we are likely to see more of in the future. Since I don't know exactly what your situation is, I've kept these fairly general. Read them, digest them and then work through the self-coaching questions at the end of the section in order to develop an appraisal of your own set of circumstances.

1. **The composition of organisations is changing**. Charles Handy, the famous business development guru, predicted in his book *The Age of Unreason* that the organisation of the future would have three main components: core professional staff; temporary, part-time and occasional staff; and external contractors brought in for short-term pieces of work. When you think of your own possible role in an organisation (or in your own business) which of these types of working role resonates most strongly with you?

2. **We are seeing the rise of the "virtual organisation"**. Home

working, teleworking, hot-desking and constant contact through email and the internet mean that the office environment many of us have been used to is becoming a thing of the past. Our lives are becoming increasingly influenced by e-business, with the power of the digital world doubling every six months. Increasingly, our mobile phones are becoming linked to commerce. You can now scan the barcodes in magazine and billboard adverts in order to discover the price of a particular item and the nearest place you can buy it.

3. **A gulf will appear between different "styles" of organisation.** Some organisations will maintain a more "traditional" structure and set of working arrangements (e.g. paper-based systems), but workers will be required to either make a choice or get used to navigating between the two. This is where your environment quadrant comes to the fore (see Chapter 4).

4. **The fastest growing job markets are in sales, customer services, computing and information-based industries.** However, many of these are considered "non-core" functions, which can be outsourced. Much of this work will be done by home workers.

5. **Prospective employees expect to have a variety of experiences.** It's not uncommon now for people to leave permanent jobs for short-term jobs if they feel that these offer an opportunity for them to grow their skills and experience significantly. This trend has slowed somewhat in the wake of the recession.

Most of the jobs our children will undertake have not yet been created, according to John Lees, author of *How to Get a Job You'll Love*. He points out that *"traditional careers advice asked school leavers to focus on skill-shortage areas. Such advice is now dangerous, since the market changes so quickly. Workers who have just got used to … 'portfolio' experiences will have to move on to learn adaptability as their primary skill"*. (Lees, 2011 edition, p. 162)

How to Respond: Developing Yourself for the Future

In considering the trends noted above, it's clear that the following are key skills which will be necessary for any successful job-hunter, career-changer or employee:

- Adaptability

- Resilience

- Imagination

- Career-management (another reason the Vital Vocation process is your new best friend!)

- Self-reliance

- Anticipation of future trends

- Coaching

- Self-coaching

- Multi-tasking

- Taking calculated risks

- Goal creation and attainment

- Inventiveness

- Creative thinking

- Emotional intelligence

- Vision

In most cases, you won't have to acquire these skills from scratch. You need to hone your existing skills and look for opportunities to develop any you don't currently have. Work through these questions as a way of developing your own plan for ensuring you have the skills of the future.

 ## Self-Coaching Questions

1. What can you do within your current job to create opportunities for you to develop new, future-focused skills? How will you arrange this?

2. What opportunities exist within your current workplace to expand your work portfolio?

3. How can you repackage your past achievements, life experience and your unique background, in a way that describes your ability to adapt to the needs of the future?

4. How au fait are you with e-working? What can you do now to bring yourself fully up to speed?

5. What training do you need to access (online or otherwise) to round-out your package of skills and abilities?

6. What support can you ask for from others to help you through this process? Whose help will you enlist first?

How to be the CEO of You

William Bridges, author of *Jobshift*, argues that the key to career development and growth is to envision yourself as a business: a centre for profit making, ideas, and adding value. I agree with him 100% and that's one of the reasons I created the Vital Vocation process. Take some time to work through the following exercise to establish how close you are to this mind-set, making notes in your journal as you go.

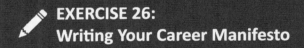

EXERCISE 26:
Writing Your Career Manifesto

Step 1

Answer the following questions:

1. What specific and unique product or service are *you* offering to your organisation or the world (including ideas, coaching, managing relationships or generally adding value)?

2. What organisational or world needs does that activity fulfil?

3. In what way is the offering uniquely *yours*? What do

you bring to it that no one else can? (You may want to review your "talents" at this point.)

4. How will you continue to create and deliver what you have to offer?

5. Why do you think that what you have to offer is a better match to your organisation's or the world's needs than similar products or services from other suppliers, internal or external?

6. What will you do to continually renew your ability to deliver what you alone can offer?

Step 2

Use the answers to write a statement which sets out your approach to the world of work from this day forward. What is it you're going to stand for in your life and career? What *won't* you stand for? See this as the best possible positive affirmation you could ever come up with – one that affirms *you* and who you really are.

Loving the Job You're in Until You Find the Job You Love

The process of finding your Vital Vocation can be exciting, exhilarating and richly rewarding. However, you may need to keep earning a living at a job you hate while you look for that vocation and that can be tough. If that's the case, you are where you are and you may as well make the most of it – and get the most from it – while it continues. Here are some pointers towards helping you make the most of your current situation:

1. **Don't forget about the "good enough job".** I defined this in Chapter 1 as being a job which may only use some of your ancillary skills (as opposed to your favourite skills or inherent talents), but which isn't toxic and doesn't take up too much of

your time. That way, you can earn your keep and use your free time to pursue a Vital Vocation. Don't automatically consider a job that fits this bill as being a bad job. The only thing that should be wrong with a good-enough job is that it isn't quite enough to completely fulfil you. If that's *all* that's wrong with your job, that's great – because it can be a terrific springboard to your ideal work.

2. **Recognise when you really must get out.** If your job *is* toxic and *does* take up too much of your time, you really do need to get out. Start looking for alternatives and be prepared to move to a "good-enough job" first, before you set your sights on you Vital Vocation (and bear in mind that a "good enough job" plus the pursuit of the things you love *is* a Vital Vocation).

3. **Make the most of job development opportunities.** Even in a job that's not ideal, there are likely to be opportunities to develop yourself in ways that will be useful in the future, once you're in a job that you *do* enjoy. In fact, such on-the-job self-development is likely to help you find a better job.

   Look for corporate training schemes that you could enrol in. Some companies will allocate each member of staff a training budget which they can spend on in-house training programmes, or even on external training opportunities. If such resources are available to you, make sure to avail yourself of them.

   If these resources aren't available, look for your own opportunities – night classes, distance-learning courses and the full range of fantastic online learning that's available now. There are also some great free online learning websites, such as TED Talks (http://www.ted.com/talks) and Annenberg Learner (http://www.learner.org/).

4. **Explore creative career options from where you are.** Even if the job you're in isn't where you want to be, it may offer you some useful flexibility. As the economic situation bites, many companies are looking for ways to save some money. Staff members who are willing to be flexible are suddenly in greater demand. If you hate your job because it's too pressurised, would you be willing to take a post at a lower level? Of course, there will be implications for your salary, but many people find that

less stress is more than a fair trade off for less money.

Some companies also offer the opportunity of secondments into different jobs within the company (or into similar jobs in other companies). This could be worth exploring if you want to get a sense of what life would be like in a different working situation. Another option for many is an unpaid sabbatical – a substantial period away from the workplace which, for those who can afford it, can be a great way of gaining a new perspective. Some people use sabbaticals to travel or to undertake some creative endeavour (like writing a book). You might want to use it to begin the process of finding your Vital Vocation.

5. **Use your free time wisely.** Your job might feel like the worst in the world, but it's likely that it still affords you a considerable amount of free time each week. If so, then don't just use that time to slump in front of the TV feeling miserable. Diarise some "Vital Vocation sessions" into your diary and use them to work through the process outlined in this book.

It's the first step towards a whole new life…

Always you have been told that work is
a curse and labour a misfortune.
But I say to you that when you work
you fulfil a part of earth's furthest dream, assigned
to you when that dream was born,
And in keeping yourself with labour
you are in truth loving life,
And to love life through labour is to be
intimate with life's inmost secret.

~ Kahlil Gibran, *On Work*

AFTERWORD
QUESTIONS AND ANSWERS

I hope I've presented you with a process that you've found immediately useful in helping you chart your own course to a better life and a happier career. I hope it's a process you'll keep close to you throughout your working life, so that you can use it again the next time you need to make a positive career change or recalibration.

My greatest hope of all is that you actually put the contents of this book into practice, so that you can enjoy what so many of us are able to enjoy on a daily basis: the pure pleasure of your very own Vital Vocation.

To close, I'm going to present you with some of the questions I'm regularly asked by coaching clients, workshop participants and blog readers, and the answers I've given them. Hopefully, you'll find something of value in these answers, too.

I think I've discovered my Vital Vocation, but it isn't anything particularly world-changing. Won't it be awfully selfish of me to pursue it?

It might actually be more selfish of you *not* to pursue it. Who knows what good it will do in the world? At least there will be one more happy, fulfilled person doing what they love and it seems to me that that's a good thing. There are really only two things to bear in mind here. Firstly, you don't *know* if it's going to be world-changing or not. Even if it doesn't seem that way on the surface, there's no telling who or what your work might inspire in the future. Secondly, whoever said a Vital Vocation *had* to be world-changing? The only world it really needs to change is your own. If you've found what you love doing, it will lead to a happier life.

Why do you place so much emphasis on finding talents first? Once I get to the job, won't I still need to learn specific skills?

You will and that's exactly the point – you can *learn* skills, if you need them. Talents are inherent. You can't teach yourself to be talented at something, but with practice you can teach yourself to become more skilled at something. I've discovered that finding and using our talents is one of the surest ways of making ourselves happy. When we do what we're naturally good at, we feel comfortable, focused and sometimes even joyful. It makes sense to build our jobs or businesses around our talents, because at least then we know the core of our work is going to be something that really matters to us. If we need skills to support that work, we can either learn them or hire others who possess them.

I've heard that people who love their work experience passion or bliss on a regular basis. I never seem to feel that way. Is there something wrong with me?

Absolutely not. Finding your Vital Vocation doesn't guarantee that you're going to float around on Cloud 9 feeling like you're blazing with inspiration. Everyone is different and some of us don't seem to experience such extreme emotions (although emotions are such subjective things, it's really impossible to tell). What finding your Vital Vocation *can* provide you with is a combination of feelings that are much more attainable and, in my opinion, valuable: a sense of focus, enthusiasm, a feeling of pleasurable absorption, a belief in the value of your work, plain old *enjoyment*. These are underrated experiences and, sadly, too few workers today have them.

I'm in a really bad place financially. I have so many debts I'm nearly paralysed with fear. Is it really a good time to start looking for my Vital Vocation?

There may be no better time, but let's be clear: finding your ideal career and sorting out your financial situation are really two different issues, although they may of course be connected. If you're in debt, you need to sort that out so that it doesn't interfere with your enjoyment of life or your ability to focus on improving your work situation.

Take a look at Chapter 9 again, particularly the section on *Getting Your Finances onto a Sure Footing*. Get help and advice if you need to. Make dealing with your debts a priority; there are many different ways to do this and support *is* available. It may be that you need to take some action on this first so that you can get on with finding your Vital Vocation, unencumbered by worry. But you may also find that looking for your Vital Vocation *while* you're dealing with your debts is a perfect way of making yourself feel more in control of the situation and taking your mind off your money worries.

I'm an introvert and very shy; will this process still work for me?

Of course! Whether you're an introvert or an extrovert, you can find your Vital Vocation. I'm an introvert myself, and in my client base, I have a mixture of extroverts, introverts and in-between-verts (that's a made up term, by the way). They've all been able to use this process to great effect. In fact, there are some elements of the process that introverts may find easier than extroverts, such as the soul-searching exercises in Part 1. Other elements may be slightly easier for extroverts, like phoning up and making enquiries about potential job opportunities.

Like anything, you'll find that you take to certain parts more than others. But, yes, this process can absolutely work for you. It can work for anyone, if they actually apply it! If you are really crippled by shyness then you may need some support during parts of the process. Consider hiring a coach or working with a friend on the more difficult parts. And if there are parts that are too hard for you at first, then just do what you can and keep moving forward. I think you'll be surprised at how much progress you make.

I think I know what I want to do, but I really *really* don't think it's possible for me to get there – the obstacles are just too great. What do I do now?

You stop believing that the obstacles are too great. You're going to go on feeling that way as long as your mind remains closed to the possibility of something else. I'm not belittling how you feel – believe me, I understand it. That's why I spent some considerable time outlining ways to deal with internal obstacles in Chapter 8, and external obstacles in Chapters 10 and 11. Forget about the *scale* of your perceived obstacles. Think more about what *kind* they are. Reread those chapters, do the relevant exercises and keep moving forward. Trust the process. Remember, although not all obstacles can be removed, they can all be got round or over if you do some investigating and really take a look at *all* your options (including changing your perspective on the situation). I repeat - trust the process!

I want to get started, but I can't imagine giving up my comfortable job to do what I really love. Am I stuck?

Only if you say so. I hope I've made it clear that you don't have to give up your comfortable job to start finding and even doing what you love – at least not at first and maybe not ever. Once you discover what you love, you should start doing it – even if it's just in your spare time. It may be that what you love is something you should *only* do in your spare time (because it can't support you, or you don't want it to) and you need to find a "good-enough job" to pay the bills and put food on the table.

Believing that we can't find what we love because we can't give up our current comfortable job (or lifestyle) is just one of the ways we stop ourselves from getting started. Get started on this process and see what comes up. You *never* have to give anything up you don't want to, including your current job. But you'll never know if there's a better alternative if you don't at least try. I suggest you reread Chapter 8, which is all about getting past the beliefs that keep us from moving forward.

I already know what I love. I also know that I can't make any money doing it. What should I do?

To start with, you should make money doing something else and you should *still* get on with doing what you love. Remember, your Vital Vocation and your salary *can* be connected, but they don't *have* to be. My only real interest in encouraging you to find your Vital Vocation is because I've come to see that it's what makes us happy. I don't guarantee that it'll make you rich. In fact, I don't even guarantee that it'll make you any money at all.

Happiness is what we tend to think money can buy us anyway, so why not just cut out the middle man and do the thing that makes us happiest? We need money to live, of course, and that's where the "good-enough job" comes in. Do what you need to do to keep the wolves from the door, *and* also do what you need to do to feel fulfilled in your life. Start by doing both and you may find at some point that the two start to coincide. Whether they eventually do or they don't, you can make money and you can do what you love. Win-win!

What if my dream job doesn't exist and I have to create it? Surely I'd be mad to go self-employed in this crazy economy?

I'm not going to sugar-coat it: yes, it's tough out there. There are risks in going self-employed or setting up your own business. Chapter 14 will help you discover if you have what it takes and if you decide you *do*, then you may want to think about the help and support you need. Coaching and mentoring from someone who has already walked that path might be helpful. And again, you can always start building up your business in your spare time, while you still have a day-job to support you.

If you *don't* have a day-job to support you, it may be a priority to get one. Don't forget about the "good-enough job" here, either. A job that pays the bills and leaves you with enough time to pursue your dream is, in my opinion, a just-about-perfect job. The only thing wrong with it is that it's not quite *enough*. Use the free time and security it gives you to go after the "enough".

What's with the elephant on the cover?

Funnily enough, you're not the first person to ask that. I chose it as a possible cover image because I loved it as soon as I saw it and felt it really stood out – always useful when you're trying to get people to notice your book! Then I gave my blog readers and social media followers the chance to vote on this image or an alternative version of the cover. The elephant won hands down, and it seems that the people who liked it did so for many different reasons.

Some saw this beautiful creature as a symbol of strength, wisdom and purpose. Some saw the tightrope it was walking along as a sign of the balancing act we all must perform on the quest to our ideal work. Some felt the umbrella was an indicator of hope and representative of the tools we need to help us along the way, especially if we fall. One person told me the image made him think of the precarious nature of the job market nowadays, while another said it made her feel like anything was possible if we're using our talents. Some people see the elephant as unhappy and in desperate need of careers advice. Meanwhile, others feel this is an elephant that has clearly found its Vital Vocation!

I love the image because it seems to say exactly what each observer needs it to say, and that feels right for a book that's all about charting our own individual path to the work we love. So – what does the elephant say to *you?*

Once I find my Vital Vocation, does that mean I'll never have a bad day at work again?

Oh, if only! No – finding your Vital Vocation is a great and fulfilling thing, but after you've found it, you're still going to be in the real world. I love my career, but I still have difficult, messy, frustrating, even infuriating days – sometimes several of them in a row. The difference is that because I've built my working life around my talents, values, skills and environmental considerations – my Vital Vocation – the good days far outweigh the bad and the bad days are still more than worth it.

I no longer find myself thinking "why am I wasting my time doing this?" because I always *know* why I'm doing what I do: because I love it and because it gives me a sense of real satisfaction. The worst of the bad days on your Vital Vocation will seem like a cakewalk compared to the best of the bad days in a job you hate.

That's what makes this journey so worth taking.

Bon voyage!

Twenty years from now, you will be more disappointed by the things you didn't do than by the things you did. So throw off the bowlines. Sail away from the safe harbour. Catch the trade winds in your sails. Explore. Dream. Discover.

~ Mark Twain

STAY IN TOUCH

If you want to get an automatic email when my next book is released sign up at http://www.cormackcarr.com/list. Your email address will never be shared and you can can unsubscribe at any time. You'll also get a free copy of my e-booklet 'The Top 10 Best & Worst Ways To Find A New Job'.

USEFUL RESOURCES

Selected Bibliography

Far from being a comprehensive list of all the useful books that are now available, this is my selection of those I've found most useful both for myself and for my coaching clients.

Ashton, Robert; *How to be a Social Entrepreneur – Make Money and Change the World* (Capstone, 2010). Advice on how to make a difference while you're making money.

Boldt, Laurence G.; *Zen and the Art of Making a Living* (Penguin, 2009). A comprehensive and meditative approach to making money whilst staying maintaining your integrity

Bolles, Richard N.; *What Color Is Your Parachute – A Practical Manual for Job-Hunters and Career-Changers* (Ten Speed Press, 2011). A perennial classic and an in-depth guide to crafting your own career path.

Brande, Dorothea; *Becoming a Writer* (Jeremy P. Tarcher, 1981). Outlines a great way to unlock your creativity, even if you don't want to become a writer.

Bridges, William; *Creating You & Co – Be the Boss of Your Own Career* (Nicholas Brealey Publishing, 1997). A useful treatise on the importance of seeing yourself as the chief executive of your own career, no matter who you work for.

Bungay Stanier, Michael; *Do More Great Work* (Workman Publishing Company Inc., 2010). Focuses on helping us, through several innovative practices, to spend more time on the kind of work that matters and makes us feel happy.

Elkington, John and Hartigan, Pamela; *The Power of Unreasonable People: How Social Entrepreneurs Create Markets That Change The World* (Harvard Business School Press, 2008). An interesting analysis of how socially-focused organisations can make a positive difference as well as a profit.

Gelb, Michael; *How to Think Like Leonardo Da Vinci* (Element, 2004). A fascinating study of the way this famous polymath's mind worked and how you can train yours to do the same.

Hall, Alvin; *You and Your Money* (Hodder, 2012). Straightforward advice on dealing with debt and planning for your financial future.

Handy, Charles; *The Age of Unreason: New Thinking for a New World* (Random House Business, 2002). A look at how the world is changing at an increasingly rapid pace, and how this effects us in our lives and careers.

Holland, John; *Making Vocational Choices* (Psychological Assessment Resources Inc., 1997). The background thinking to the Holland Code system referred to in Chapters 3 and 4.

Horn, Sam; *What's Holding You Back?* (St. Martin's Press, 1997). A sometimes whimsical look at your own barriers and how to overcome them.

Katie, Byron and Mitchell, Stephen; *Loving What Is* (Rider, 2002). A fascinating account of one woman's experience of clarity and freedom, and the process she developed to make the same experience available to others.

Lees, John; *How to Get a Job You'll Love* (McGraw-Hill, 2001). A mixture of positively inspiring and very practical advice for landing a job that you can really enjoy.

Lewis, Ann; *Recover Your Balance – How to Bounce Back from Bad Times at Work* (Bookshaker, 2010). A straightforward and helpful look at how to recover from setbacks in the workplace.

Lore, Nicholas; *The Pathfinder – How To Choose or Change Your Career for a Lifetime of Satisfaction and Success* (Simon and Schuster, 1998). A motivational approach to finding the right career for you and balancing it with a happy life.

Owen, Grace; *The Career Itch – 4 Steps for Taking Control of What You Do Next* (OG Publishing, 2009). An experienced career coach's expert perspective on taking practical and attainable steps that help to move you forward in your career.

Rickman, Cheryl D.; *The Small Business Start-Up Workbook* (How-To Books, 2005.) Sensible and practical advice on taking the first steps into your own business.

Schepp, Brad and Debra; *How To Find a Job on LinkedIn, Facebook, Twitter and Google+* (McGraw Hill, 2012). Full of useful information on how to make the most of your social media presence whilst avoiding some of the most destructive online pitfalls.

Sher, Barbara; *It's Only Too Late if You Don't Start Now – How to Create Your Second Life at Any Age* (Dell, 1998). A no-nonsense approach to finding the work of your dreams, even if you think you're getting on a bit.

Sher, Barbara; *Refuse to Choose* (Rodale Press, 2007). If you have too many interests and can't choose between them, you could be a "scanner". Far from being a bad thing, this could be the best news you've ever heard.

Stroebel, Charles; *The Quieting Reflex* (Berkley Publishing Group, 1983.) Out-of-print but worth seeking out for a fuller explanation of this useful stress-busting technique.

Winter, Barbara J.; *Making a Living Without a Job* (Bantam Books, 2009). Join the ranks of the "joyfully jobless" with this lively guide to successful self-employment.

RECOMMENDED WEBSITES

It can be hard sometimes to sort the quality online information from all the rest. These sites will give you a great head start.

Vital Vocation:
http://www.vitalvocation.com/ My own career-coaching blog. Come and join the conversation!

Vital Vocation Facebook Page:
http://www.facebook.com/vitalvocation A place for job-hunters, career-changers and new business-builders to gather and share tips and information.

Vital Vocation on Twitter:
@vitalvocation Up-to-the minute news and information on how to find or create your ideal work. Come and say hello!

Careershifters:
http://www.careershifters.org/ A leading career-change advice service based in the UK

Top 9 Job Search Sites:
http://mashable.com/2011/01/10/job-sites-to-bookmark/ A guide to some of the most useful places to visit on the web for job-hunters, career-changers and business-builders.

Job Search Tools, Widgets and Gadgets:
http://jobsearch.about.com/od/jobsearchtips/a/widgets.htm A great place to look if you need some specific job-hunting help.

Job Search Cafe:
http://www.jobsearchcafe.com/ A social networking site for connecting with other job-hunters and career-changers.

ABOUT THE AUTHOR

Brian Cormack Carr is a writer, certified career coach and chief executive of BVSC The Centre for Voluntary Action, one of the UK's leading charities. He trained in personnel management with Marks & Spencer plc and gained an MA (Hons) in English Literature and Language from the University of Aberdeen.

Brian has nearly 20 years experience in the fields of personal development and leadership, and has helped hundreds of clients, readers and workshop participants to find fulfilling work and a renewed sense of purpose.

On the path to his own Vital Vocation, he has experienced a wide range of interesting jobs, having been: a residential social worker in a care home for young adults with challenging behaviours; a maker of plastic bus-stop shelters; a courier and lab technician for a granary; and an ironmonger's shop assistant. He remembers each one as a privilege and an education.

He even tried his hand (as a student) at selling double glazing through telesales – but only lasted for one day after being tormented by feelings of guilt and calling all of his prospects back to tell them that they weren't actually obliged to buy anything. His boss wasn't very pleased. He has since chalked that one up to experience.

Brian's base on the web is <u>www.cormackcarr.com</u> where you can find out more about his work and all his forthcoming publications.